S0-BRM-226

Devotions to Go

ZONDERVAN®
.com

ZONDERVAN

Devotions to Go, Volume One
Copyright © 2009 by Zondervan

Requests for information should be addressed to:
Zondervan, *Grand Rapids, Michigan 49530*

ISBN 978-0-310-82280-6

Content excerpted from *The New Women's Devotional Bible*, Copyright© 2006, Zondervan, and *The Couple's Devotional Bible*, Copyright© 2008, Zondervan. Used by permission. All Scripture quotations, unless otherwise indicated, are taken from the Holy Bible, New International Version®. NIV®. Copyright© 1973, 1978, 1984 by International Bible Society. Used by permission of Zondervan. All rights reserved.

Any Internet addresses (websites, blogs, etc.) and telephone numbers printed in this book are offered as a resource. They are not intended in any way to be or imply an endorsement by Zondervan, nor does Zondervan vouch for the content of these sites and numbers for the life of this book.

Interior design by Steve Culver

Printed in China

---

09 10 11 12 13 14 15 • 23 22 21 20 19 18 17 16 15 14 13 12 11 10 9 8 7 6 5 4 3 2 1

Volume One

Daniel 1:8-16

Daniel resolved not to defile himself with the royal food and wine, and he asked the chief official for permission not to defile himself this way. Now God had caused the official to show favor and sympathy to Daniel, but the official told Daniel, "I am afraid of my LORD the king, who has assigned your food and drink. Why should he see you looking worse than the other young men your age? The king would then have my head because of you."

Daniel then said to the guard whom the chief official had appointed over Daniel, Hananiah, Mishael and Azariah, "Please test your servants for ten days: Give us nothing but vegetables to eat and water to drink. Then compare our appearance with that of the young men who eat the royal food, and treat your servants in accordance with what you see." So he agreed to this and tested them for ten days.

At the end of the ten days they looked healthier and better nourished than any of the young men who ate the royal food. So the guard took away their choice food and the wine they were to drink and gave them vegetables instead.

Eating right together

Personal change, so important in marriage, is also a theme in the Old Testament. Daniel and his friends were good Jewish boys who were unwilling to give up their holy eating habits while being trained to serve in the king's palace. They politely refused to defile themselves with royal food and wine, choosing instead a simple diet of vegetables and water. And God honored them by making them look healthier and more nourished after ten days than those who ate the king's food.

God wasn't just being fussy in insisting that these young men eat only foods that were prepared according to Jewish dietary laws. He was showing them and us to make a connection between spirit and body. He was teaching them to be holy in every part of life.

Couples face big changes when they start eating together every day. Choosing what to eat may be one of the most subtle yet important changes we have to make to sustain a long life together.

Daniel and his friends risked a king's wrath and possible death for choosing the way of holiness and health. What are we willing to give up to live right before God in every part of our lives, right down to what we put in our mouths?

Psalm 116:1-6

*I love the LORD, for he heard my
voice; he heard my cry for mercy.
Because he turned his ear to me,
I will call on him as long as I live.*

*The cords of death entangled me,
the anguish of the grave came
upon me; I was overcome by
trouble and sorrow. Then I called
on the name of the LORD: "LORD,
save me!"*

*The LORD is gracious and righteous;
our God is full of compassion. The
LORD protects the simplehearted;
when I was in great need, he
saved me.*

God is faithful

Some people have an answer for most problems in life. They have a lot to say on almost any subject. But as they go through life, they often have fewer answers. There's really only one simple explanation for everything in life: God is faithful.

God won't wave a magic wand and then everything will fall into place. Far from it. But in the darkest times in our lives we will learn to keep turning our face toward him; he is faithful. Faithful to be with us, faithful to watch over us, faithful to work in us to make us the men and women we are called to be.

No matter what the circumstances are in your life right now or how fast you feel you're falling, or whether you're frozen on the bar, afraid to let go and grab hold of God's hands, God is there and he won't let you go. He will catch you in midair. The net of his faithful love will cushion you when you fall.

Mark 1:14-20

After John was put in prison, Jesus went into Galilee, proclaiming the good news of God. "The time has come," he said. "The kingdom of God is near. Repent and believe the good news!"

As Jesus walked beside the Sea of Galilee, he saw Simon and his brother Andrew casting a net into the lake, for they were fishermen. "Come, follow me," Jesus said, "and I will make you fishers of men." At once they left their nets and followed him.

When he had gone a little farther, he saw James son of Zebedee and his brother John in a boat, preparing their nets. Without delay he called them, and they left their father Zebedee in the boat with the hired men and followed him.

Follow me

Imagine being busy about your work and having someone come along and say, "Drop everything and come with me—for good!" Can you imagine that you would actually follow that command? Yet when Jesus spoke a similar command to Simon and Andrew, they dropped everything and went with him.

As Christ's disciples today, how life-changing is his call to us, "Follow me"? It can be just as life-changing for us as it was for Simon Peter and his brother, Andrew, even though the Lord may not call us to turn our backs on our life's work to become traveling evangelists.

That call, "Follow me," carries with it the command to stop following our own agenda, and that's extraordinarily counter cultural in the twenty-first century. So many voices in our society tell us to "look out for number one." But Jesus says, "Get out of the driver's seat!" It seems unrealistic to relinquish our own plans and goals and dreams to serve somebody else, but that's what Jesus wants us to do.

The good news is that our best interests are safe in God's hands. He knows our plans, goals and dreams, and he knows better than we do what is ultimately best for us.

Genesis 1:27-31

So God created man in his own image, in the image of God he created him; male and female he created them.

God blessed them and said to them, "Be fruitful and increase in number; fill the earth and subdue it. Rule over the fish of the sea and the birds of the air and over every living creature that moves on the ground."

Then God said, "I give you every seed-bearing plant on the face of the whole earth and every tree that has fruit with seed in it. They will be yours for food. And to all the beasts of the earth and all the birds of the air and all the creatures that move on the ground—everything that has the breath of life in it—I give every green plant for food." And it was so.

God saw all that he had made, and it was very good.

God's image bearers

Imagine the scene. Holding her hair back with one hand, the woman kneels and leans forward to drink from the clear pool of water. As her cupped hand reaches for the clear liquid, she draws back startled. Who is the long-haired stranger staring back at her?

Perhaps ever since the time Eve first caught sight of her reflection in the Garden of Eden, women have dealt with the question of image. Polls consistently reveal that the majority of us are dissatisfied with our appearance. Confronted with a barrage of airbrushed photos of super-models and celebrities adorning magazine covers, the average woman thinks she is too short, too fat, too unattractive, too imperfect. How can we ever measure up with the media's standards of perfection?

The first chapter of the Bible supplies the answer. We were created in the image of one paradigm of perfection: our Creator. Our height, weight and skin color may indicate our human origins, but our soul and spirit reflect our Sovereign God.

God created us to convey the distinctive imprint of his divine nature to a world often blinded to his existence. Even our differences reflect the One who delighted in creating a world of dazzling diversity.

When Micaiah son of Gemariah, the son of Shaphan, heard all the words of the LORD from the scroll, he went down to the secretary's room in the royal palace, where all the officials were sitting. After Micaiah told them everything he had heard Baruch read to the people from the scroll, all the officials sent Jehudi son of Nethaniah, the son of Shelemiah, the son of Cushi, to say to Baruch, "Bring the scroll from which you have read to the people and come." So Baruch son of Neriah went to them with the scroll in his hand. They said to him, "Sit down, please, and read it to us."

When they heard all these words, they looked at each other in fear and said to Baruch, "We must report all these words to the king."

They went to the king in the courtyard and reported everything to him. The king sent Jehudi to get the scroll, and Jehudi brought it from the room of Elishama the secretary and read it to the king and all the officials standing beside him. It was the ninth month and the king was sitting in the winter apartment, with a fire burning in the firepot in front of him. Whenever Jehudi had read three or four columns of the scroll, the king cut them off with a scribe's knife and threw them into the firepot, until the entire scroll was burned in the fire.

Personal Delivery

"Put it in writing." Those four words get results. And so when God wanted to get someone's attention, that's exactly what he did: He put it in writing.

Through the prophet Jeremiah and his faithful scribe, Baruch, God dictated a personal message to King Jehoiakim and his people. While we don't know exactly what part of Jeremiah's prophecy was written down for the king, we know this much: The king didn't like it. In fact, not only did the king refuse to comply, but he treated God's words with contempt by burning the scroll piece by piece. No one in his right mind would treat the words of God in such a way, right?

And yet have you ever disrespected God's Word? Think about it. You may not torch its pages, but have you ever just ignored it? Think of God's story as a first-class letter addressed to you. Think of his words as intimate and deeply personal—something he wants you to know, something straight from his heart. When God had something important to say, he could have used a number of means to communicate it. But he chose to put it in writing. Find a quiet, cozy corner and open His "letter." Find out what he wants to say to you personally.

2 Kings 20:1-6; 21:1-6

In those days Hezekiah became ill and was at the point of death. The prophet Isaiah son of Amoz went to him and said, "This is what the LORD says: Put your house in order, because you are going to die; you will not recover."

Hezekiah turned his face to the wall and prayed to the LORD, "Remember, O LORD, how I have walked before you faithfully and with wholehearted devotion and have done what is good in your eyes." And Hezekiah wept bitterly.

Before Isaiah had left the middle court, the word of the LORD came to him: "Go back and tell Hezekiah, the leader of my people, 'This is what the LORD, the God of your father David, says: "I have heard your prayer and seen your tears; I will heal you. On the third day from now you will go up to the temple of the LORD. I will add fifteen years to your life.' "

Manasseh was twelve years old when he became king, and he reigned in Jerusalem fifty-five years. His mother's name was Hephzibah. He did evil in the eyes of the LORD, following the detestable practices of the nations the LORD had driven out before the Israelites. He rebuilt the high places his father Hezekiah had destroyed; he also erected altars to Baal and made an Asherah pole, as Ahab king of Israel had done. He bowed down to all the starry hosts and worshiped them. He sacrificed his own son in the fire, practiced sorcery and divination, and consulted mediums and spiritists. He did much evil in the eyes of the LORD, provoking him to anger.

When time runs out

I f you knew you had fifteen years to live, how would you spend your remaining time on earth? Watching TV? Eating more ice cream? Spending more time with each other? Buying more stuff? Having a child?

King Hezekiah did the equivalent of all that. When he was told he was about to die but then had that sentence amended to include fifteen more years of life, he took his medicine, got out of bed and went back to work. And he had a son, Manasseh.

If Hezekiah had not lived those extra fifteen years, the course of Israel's history would have been different. Manasseh became king when he was twelve years old and ruled for fifty-five years. During that time he undid all the good his father had done.

The sins of our children aren't always a direct result of our parenting, but often they are. It's a pretty sure guess that Hezekiah didn't wisely use the time with his son during the final fifteen years of his life. Time is easily squandered, yet it's impossible to get it back. Time is especially precious when children are involved, and it's sobering to know that they learn the value of time and of life by our example.

"I loathe my very life; therefore I will give free rein to my
complaint and speak out in
the bitterness of my soul.

I will say to God: Do not
condemn me, but tell me what
charges you have against me.

Does it please you to oppress
me, to spurn the work of your
hands, while you smile on the
schemes of the wicked?

Do you have eyes of flesh? Do
you see as a mortal sees?

Are your days like those of a mortal
or your years like those of a man,
that you must search out my
faults and probe after my sin—

though you know that I am
not guilty and that no one can
rescue me from your hand?

Your hands shaped me and
made me. Will you now
turn and destroy me?

Remember that you molded
me like clay. Will you now
turn me to dust again?

"Why then did you bring me
out of the womb? I wish I had
died before any eye saw me.

If only I had never come into
being, or had been carried straight
from the womb to the grave!"

Turning bitterness to joy

*L*ike Job, Martin knew what it was like to wish he was dead. Death seemed preferable to facing the wreck his marriage to Charlene had become. Things had been bad for years—a sort of dull bad—but now Martin realized he felt a deep sadness about his marriage. And, he'd kept that locked up.

Initially, Martin hesitated to follow Job's example to give free rein to his complaint and speak out in the bitterness of his soul, since even voicing his hurt to God would have required being honest with himself. But one morning, sitting with his Bible and reading the book of Job, Martin cracked. All his feelings came pouring out, and God listened.

That talk with God prompted lots of other conversations—with Charlene and with their new counselor. Martin says that through those conversations he's learned a lot about himself and his wife, about forgiveness and reconciliation. But most important, he says, he has learned to be honest with God.

Hopefully, you've not been in a marriage as heartbreaking as Martin's—and certainly your life has not been as tragic as Job's—but maybe you too have been so bitterly disappointed in your marriage that you've fantasized about checking out. But you don't have to bear the disappointment alone. Talk to God and allow him to bear it with you.

A woman whose little daughter was possessed by an evil spirit came to fall at Jesus' feet.

She begged Jesus to drive the demon out of her daughter.

"First let the children eat all they want," he told her, "for it is not right to take the children's bread and toss it to their dogs."

"Yes, Lord," she replied, "but even the dogs under the table eat the children's crumbs."

Then Jesus told her, "For such a reply, you may go; the demon has left your daughter."

A strong-willed woman

So what does it take to have the distinction of being a genuinely strong-willed woman? After all, every woman has opportunities to use some degree of strong will at various times in her life. But for those of us who fit the description of the strong-willed woman, it can be said that we use our strong wills almost as often as we breathe.

Take Emily who wondered if it's possible for a strong-willed woman to be a Christian. She confessed that she had very deliberately stayed away from church the last few years because she knew she had a stubborn and independent nature. Half of her was afraid God wouldn't want her, and the other half was afraid he would demand she give up her strong will.

Emily is certainly not alone. There are many strong-willed women whose hearts and souls long to know Christ, but whose self-sufficient natures won't even consider the possibility of surrendering their hard-won independence. These are women who change the world one way or another. It's never been more important for them to find a way to validate their worth in the kingdom of God. So let's come together and let's discover and celebrate the fact that God has placed in the heart of many of his human creations an undercurrent so strong and so solid that it carries us from birth to death.

17

When the people saw that Moses was so long in coming down from the mountain, they gathered around Aaron and said, "Come, make us gods who will go before us. As for this fellow Moses who brought us up out of Egypt, we don't know what has happened to him."

Aaron answered them, "Take off the gold earrings that your wives, your sons and your daughters are wearing, and bring them to me." So all the people took off their earrings and brought them to Aaron. He took what they handed him and made it into an idol cast in the shape of a calf, fashioning it with a tool. Then they said, "These are your gods, O Israel, who brought you up out of Egypt."

When Aaron saw this, he built an altar in front of the calf and announced, "Tomorrow there will be a festival to the LORD." So the next day the people rose early and sacrificed burnt offerings and presented fellowship offerings. Afterward they sat down to eat and drink and got up to indulge in revelry.

Gold or God?

I dolatry is alive and well in the modern world. People worship at the temple of self. They bow down to the god of money. They make sacrifices to elusive dreams of perfection—the perfect husband, the perfect family, the perfect body, the perfect life. Perfection becomes a substitute for the gold and jewels the Israelites used to create idols.

You may not think you're guilty of idol worship. You wouldn't bow down to an animal figurine. You go to church every Sunday. You have a Bible sitting on your bedside table. But do you long for a golden dream you can fashion to your own whims?

Our golden dreams of earthly perfection encapsulate only what we allow; they stay as safe as we like them, as shimmering and domestic as we dare. God is wild, unsafe, unpredictable even. He does not fit into the neat fairy tale we sometimes prefer over him.

So what do you turn to when God feels untamed? The golden dream will not soothe your soul. The illusion of perfection does not comfort you when you mourn. Gold will not go with you into eternity. But God can, and will, do all these things when you worship him "in spirit and in truth" (John 4:24).

19

Solomon gave orders to build a temple for the Name of the LORD and a royal palace for himself. He conscripted seventy thousand men as carriers and eighty thousand as stonecutters in the hills and thirty-six hundred as foremen over them.

Solomon sent this message to Hiram king of Tyre: "Send me cedar logs as you did for my father David when you sent him cedar to build a palace to live in. Now I am about to build a temple for the Name of the LORD my God and to dedicate it to him for burning fragrant incense before him, for setting out the consecrated bread regularly, and for making burnt offerings every morning and evening and on Sabbaths and New Moons and at the appointed feasts of the LORD our God. This is a lasting ordinance for Israel.

"The temple I am going to build will be great, because our God is greater than all other gods. But who is able to build a temple for him, since the heavens, even the highest heavens, cannot contain him? Who then am I to build a temple for him, except as a place to burn sacrifices before him?"

Something beautiful for God

It's not wrong to want something for yourself—as long as you don't cling too tightly to it. When it comes to sharing, the fair split goes, "One for you, one for me."

Solomon had plenty of possessions, and he was generous and played fair. A temple for God, a palace for himself. Do you know someone who's done the same? They have the money to build a nice house for themselves, and they also fund a church project or a center for the homeless. We can be encouraged by their example and by Solomon's example.

God doesn't need our things. But he ordains our work and endows us with creativity and talent. He designed us to be busy about the business of doing things for him, of making all kinds of things that reflect his regenerating grace and that glorify him.

In what beautiful enterprise might God be directing you to be involved? It could be people or projects, aptitudes or art. Find the helpers and materials needed to accomplish your goal. Go ahead and enjoy the process and the fruit of your labor, like Solomon did. But give fairly and generously to the author of your gifts and talents. Do a God-sized work for him.

The LORD said to Samuel, "How long will you mourn for Saul, since I have rejected him as king over Israel? Fill your horn with oil and be on your way; I am sending you to Jesse of Bethlehem. I have chosen one of his sons to be king."

When they arrived, Samuel saw Eliab and thought, "Surely the LORD's anointed stands here before the LORD."

But the LORD said to Samuel, "Do not consider his appearance or his height, for I have rejected him. The LORD does not look at the things man looks at. Man looks at the outward appearance, but the LORD looks at the heart."

Then Jesse called Abinadab and had him pass in front of Samuel.

But Samuel said, "The LORD has not chosen this one either. "Jesse then had Shammah pass by, but Samuel said, "Nor has the LORD chosen this one." Jesse had seven of his sons pass before Samuel, but Samuel said to him, "The LORD has not chosen these." So he asked Jesse, "Are these all the sons you have?"

"There is still the youngest," Jesse answered, "but he is tending the sheep." Samuel said, "Send for him; we will not sit down until he arrives."

So he sent and had him brought in. He was ruddy, with a fine appearance and handsome features.

Then the LORD said, "Rise and anoint him; he is the one."

What we see in each other

When we look at someone's outward appearance we often fail to see what God sees. This message was clearly illustrated to John Fisher when he was speaking at a seminar. "A couple came in late, and I could see that they were in love," Fisher said. "I couldn't help but notice the woman was very attractive while the guy was a real nerd.

"What could she see in him?" Fisher wondered. From the outside this couple didn't look like a match. "Then I realized she was blind," Fisher said.

"What did she see in him? She saw everything that was important in a person. She saw love. While another woman might not have gotten past this man's unimpressive exterior, she was blind to that. She saw only his heart."

Like Samuel, we often make judgments based on what people look like. But God doesn't use looks as his criteria. He evaluates people by what's in their hearts.

Galatians 5:16-25

So I say, live by the Spirit, and you will not gratify the desires of the sinful nature. For the sinful nature desires what is contrary to the Spirit, and the Spirit what is contrary to the sinful nature. They are in conflict with each other, so that you do not do what you want. But if you are led by the Spirit, you are not under law.

The acts of the sinful nature are obvious: sexual immorality, impurity and debauchery; idolatry and witchcraft; hatred, discord, jealousy, fits of rage, selfish ambition, dissensions, factions, and envy; drunkenness, orgies, and the like. I warn you, as I did before, that those who live like this will not inherit the kingdom of God.

But the fruit of the Spirit is love, joy, peace, patience, kindness, goodness, faithfulness, gentleness and self-control. Against such things there is no law. Those who belong to Christ Jesus have crucified the sinful nature with its passions and desires. Since we live by the Spirit, let us keep in step with the Spirit.

23

Keeping in step

ike a dancer constantly tuned to the beat of the music, we must continually tune in to the voice of the Spirit and follow his lead. But, oh, how difficult it can be. The Spirit moves us to places where we might not feel comfortable. The rhythm might be too slow or too fast. Following the Spirit means resisting the urge to dance through life our way. It means relinquishing control.

Throughout the day we should ask ourselves, "Who am I being led by? My self, with its emotions, worries, pride, fears and selfishness? Or am I being led by the Holy Spirit?"

Each time we move in step with the Spirit we are saying yes to God. We're no longer bound to follow the whims of our flesh or the whispering of the evil one. We can choose to move in sync with the Spirit.

Exodus 20:18-21

When the people saw the thunder and lightning and heard the trumpet and saw the mountain in smoke, they trembled with fear. They stayed at a distance and said to Moses, "Speak to us yourself and we will listen. But do not have God speak to us or we will die."

Moses said to the people, "Do not be afraid. God has come to test you, so that the fear of God will be with you to keep you from sinning."

The people remained at a distance, while Moses approached the thick darkness where God was.

Heart troubles

S o many things can trouble our hearts. Unpaid bills. A frightening medical prognosis. Loss of a job. The death of a loved one. Upcoming surgery. An unexpected move. An argument with a close friend. A savage rumor.

The world is full of "heart troublers," and it always will be. Yet God does not want our hearts to remain troubled. And he does not expect us to deal with those troubles so much by ignoring them as by turning toward him. What suffering and persecution and pain and difficulties do is not so much make us weak, as show us we are weak. Without them, we can deceive ourselves into believing we're prizefighters. With them, we're reminded that we're not constructed to function on our own power. The trick is to allow suffering to be used as a tool to help us depend on God and not on ourselves.

When we face far worse than our worst imaginings, something unexpected and wonderful can happen. We realize that God is in control and God is good—even when bad things happen in our lives.

Even though we don't know what we might have to go through next, we know that when we let go we'll fall into the strong hands of God.

Exodus 4:24-26

At a lodging place along the way, the LORD met Moses and was about to kill him. But Zipporah took a flint knife, cut off her son's foreskin and touched Moses' feet with it. "Surely you are a bridegroom of blood to me," she said. So the LORD let him alone. (At that time she said "bridegroom of blood," referring to circumcision.)

Making peace with each other

Zipporah performed hasty surgery on her son when she realized God was about to kill her husband, Moses. While it isn't stated, evidently God was about to destroy Moses because he failed to circumcise his son. Zipporah took the situation into her own hands, completing the act of obedience Moses had neglected to do.

But there seems to be an air of resentment in this wife's abrupt actions. Perhaps she was angry at her husband for shirking his fatherly duties. Whatever the details of a disagreement, resulting feelings can drive a wedge between spouses.

When you notice disagreement creeping in or a disagreement escalating in your relationship, admit your anger and call an immediate cease-fire. Agree on a specific time when you can talk. Then sit down together and use a small object, such as a pen, to indicate who has the floor. When the pen changes hands, the roles change. The speaker's job is to get his or her point across. The listener's job is to absorb information and give feedback by paraphrasing what the other has just said.

Very often, resentment grows from unmet expectations. Zipporah expected something from Moses. Recognizing what your expectations are is the first step toward resolving resentment.

Isaiah 25:1; 6-9

O Lord, you are my God;
I will exalt you and praise your name,
for in perfect faithfulness
you have done marvelous things,
things planned long ago.

On this mountain the Lord
Almighty will prepare
a feast of rich food for all peoples,
a banquet of aged wine—
the best of meats and the finest
of wines.

On this mountain he will destroy
the shroud that enfolds all peoples,
the sheet that covers all nations;

He will swallow up death forever.
The Sovereign Lord will wipe away
the tears from all faces;
he will remove the disgrace
of his people
from all the earth.
The Lord has spoken.

In that day they will say,
"Surely this is our God;
we trusted in him, and he saved us.
This is the Lord, we trusted in him;
let us rejoice and be glad in
his salvation."

Thank you

*D*espite all the promises and reminders, sometimes the stain of our sin seems so repugnant and the gift of God's grace seems so extravagant that we can hardly believe he bestows it on us ruined sinners so freely. But he does. His Word tells us, "If we confess our sins, he is faithful and just and will forgive us our sins and purify us from all unrighteousness."

Still, we sometimes find ourselves asking, "Lord, did we hear you right? Did you say all unrighteousness? Do you mean all my sin, past, present, and future? Even if it's a sin I find little and insignificant, like gossip; or medium-sized, like losing my temper; or great big, like murder and adultery and stealing? Did you really mean all my sin is forgiven?"

Then we hear him whispering to our hearts, "You have been made holy through the sacrifice of the body of Jesus Christ once for all."

Hearing these words we cry out in gratitude, "Thank you! Thank you! Thank you!"

Revelation 20:11-15

Then I saw a great white throne and him who was seated on it. Earth and sky fled from his presence, and there was no place for them. And I saw the dead, great and small, standing before the throne, and books were opened. Another book was opened, which is the book of life. The dead were judged according to what they had done as recorded in the books. The sea gave up the dead that were in it, and death and Hades gave up the dead that were in them, and each person was judged according to what he had done. Then death and Hades were thrown into the lake of fire. The lake of fire is the second death. If anyone's name was not found written in the book of life, he was thrown into the lake of fire.

The book of life

The day of Christ will be a great and terrible day. Great for the righteous and terrible for the unrighteous. For those who turn their backs on Christ, there is no heaven. Yes, there is a hell.

Hell is not heaven's counterpart. Heaven has no counterpart. It has no opposite. Just as Satan is not God's opposite (for the devil is merely a created being—and a fallen one, at that!), neither does heaven have an opposite. In the vastness of God's infinite as well as cleansed and purified universe, hell may end up being only a speck. A trash heap. A garbage dump.

Rather than debate the census figures of heaven and hell, it is simply sufficient to say that hell exists; it's horrible, you don't want to go there, and you want to do everything in your power to keep others from choosing it. Jesus' teaching about hell with its wormwood and gall is meant to strike terror in our hearts, warning us that if heaven is better than we could dream, so hell will be worse than we can imagine.

Hell warns us to seek heaven. It is its own best deterrent.

Moses heard the people of every family wailing, each at the entrance to his tent. The Lord became exceedingly angry, and Moses was troubled. He asked the Lord, "Why have you brought this trouble on your servant? What have I done to displease you that you put the burden of all these people on me? Did I conceive all these people? Did I give them birth? Why do you tell me to carry them in my arms, as a nurse carries an infant, to the land you promised on oath to their forefathers? Where can I get meat for all these people? They keep wailing to me, 'Give us meat to eat!' I cannot carry all these people by myself; the burden is too heavy for me. If this is how you are going to treat me, put me to death right now—if I have found favor in your eyes—and do not let me face my own ruin."

The Lord said to Moses: "Bring me seventy of Israel's elders who are known to you as leaders and officials among the people. Have them come to the Tent of Meeting, that they may stand there with you. I will come down and speak with you there, and I will take of the Spirit that is on you and put the Spirit on them. They will help you carry the burden of the people so that you will not have to carry it alone."

The light of his love

We all need an encourager—a voice that cheers you on to believe that God is who he says he is and that walking in his ways will prosper your soul. There's a lot at stake. To complicate matters, the voices that offer false promises are too alluring to refuse.

No wonder God told us to whisper the truth in each other's ears, because sin is deceitful. It lies. It makes promises it can never deliver in the long run. Initially, sin feels good. An affair is exhilarating. Controlling others is empowering. Taking revenge feels therapeutic. Fighting for our rights massages the pain of unfairness. The list goes on.

The longer we choose to believe (and act on) the false promises of sin, the harder our heart becomes. If we sin today, we will be more hardened tomorrow. We'll be even less likely to be affected by the truth. God's voice will be more unwelcome. The purity of his ways will seem more perverted.

Let's put our arms around someone who is struggling with critical choices today. Let's remind them that God's ways are worth it. He delivers what he promises: peace, confidence, eternal rewards and the joy of living in the light of his love.

2 Samuel 22:1-4

David sang to the LORD the words of this song when the LORD delivered him from the hand of all his enemies and from the hand of Saul. He said: "The LORD is my rock, my fortress and my deliverer; my God is my rock, in whom I take refuge, my shield and the horn of my salvation. He is my stronghold, my refuge and my savior— from violent men you save me. I call to the LORD, who is worthy of praise, and I am saved from my enemies.

Lifted up

*L*ife sends all kinds of storms: Financial struggles. Wayward children. The death of a loved one. Broken relationships. These events whip through our lives with gale-force winds and leave us feeling shattered, powerless and adrift like victims of a mighty tempest.

Engulfed by the floods of life and surrounded by his enemies, David was in a vulnerable place. But he remained strong because he knew the One who could bring triumph out of tragedy and victory from defeat. David trusted his mighty Savior because their relationship rested on a rock-solid, centuries-old covenant that could not be swayed. Like a small child enveloped by his parents' love, David expected God to intervene. His hopes were not in vain. God reached down and pulled David from the depths.

The One who rescued David still waits for his people to call on him during whatever trials they face. The God who lifted David to new heights and gave him a song to sing wants to reach down from on high to lift your spirits and help you rise above your circumstances.

What can you do when the storm breaks? Follow David's lead and run to God. Look to God to regenerate your strength.

Psalm 37:1-7, 9, 11

37

Do not fret because of evil men or be envious of those who do wrong; for like the grass they will soon wither, like green plants they will soon die away.

Trust in the Lord and do good; dwell in the land and enjoy safe pasture.

Delight yourself in the Lord and he will give you the desires of your heart.

Commit your way to the Lord; trust in him and he will do this:

He will make your righteousness shine like the dawn, the justice of your cause like the noonday sun.

Be still before the Lord and wait patiently for him; do not fret when men succeed in their ways, when they carry out their wicked schemes.

For evil men will be cut off, but those who hope in the Lord will inherit the land.

The meek will inherit the land and enjoy great peace.

It's not fair!

Almost everyone at one time or another has experienced a situation where they find themselves saying, "That's not fair!" The psalmist faced such a situation when he saw his enemies prosper while he suffered. David, however, turned his focus to God; he found hope in knowing that God would set things right. What was the path David took to finding peace in the midst of injustice?

- "Trust in the Lord." Every event in our lives—good and bad—is filtered through God's sovereign hands. We can trust God to use for our own good anything that others intend as evil.

- "Do good." Whatever happens, despite the injustices that we suffer, we are to choose the higher path that demonstrates God's Spirit within us.

- "Dwell in the land." Though we may feel like running away from conflict or trying to hide from challenges, doing so robs us of experiencing how God can provide a place of rest and safety.

- "Delight yourself in the Lord." Rather than getting depressed about our tough situation, turning our thoughts to God's presence and singing his praise songs will lift our spirits.

- "Commit your way to the Lord." Follow him no matter what others do or say.

- "Be still before the Lord." We can afford a lifetime of patience, for we know that God will make things right.

The kingdom of heaven is like treasure hidden in a field. When a man found it, he hid it again, and then in his joy went and sold all he had and bought that field.

The kingdom of heaven is like a merchant looking for fine pearls. When he found one of great value, he went away and sold everything he had and bought it.

The kingdom of heaven is like a net that was let down into the lake and caught all kinds of fish. When it was full, the fishermen pulled it up on the shore. Then they sat down and collected the good fish in baskets, but threw the bad away. This is how it will be at the end of the age. The angels will come and separate the wicked from the righteous and throw them into the fiery furnace, where there will be weeping and gnashing of teeth.

"Have you understood all these things?" Jesus asked. "Yes," they replied.

He said to them, "Therefore every teacher of the law who has been instructed about the kingdom of heaven is like the owner of a house who brings out of his storeroom new treasures as well as old."

Buried treasure

A re you digging for buried treasure? If not, you should know that it's waiting there for you.

But wait. Don't reach for a shovel just yet. For this kind of digging, you need other kinds of tools: your Bible, a concordance and maybe a reliable commentary or two. And bring along your mind, heart, time and a bit of patience. You may ask, "What kind of treasure can I find with these tools?" The answer is profound. You'll find a wealth of God's wisdom that can only be found when you search for it as if you were digging for gold or silver buried beneath the earth's surface.

In Matthew 11 and 12, Jesus had pronounced judgment on the unrepentant and especially the religious leaders who were uniting against him. But in Matthew 13, Jesus changed his approach in speaking to the crowds. He started teaching in parables—earthly stories with heavenly meanings. Only those who wanted to dig deep enough could understand what he was really saying. Others might pass Christ's teachings off as simple stories. But these "simple stories" were eternal stories—helping generations understand spiritual principles through physical metaphors.

Jesus gladly answered his disciples' questions about his parables. His hidden truths are an open secret for those who are really looking.

Jeremiah 29:4-7; 10-14

*This is what the L*ORD *Almighty, the God of Israel, says to all those I carried into exile from Jerusalem to Babylon: "Build houses and settle down; plant gardens and eat what they produce. Marry and have sons and daughters; find wives for your sons and give your daughters in marriage, so that they too may have sons and daughters. Increase in number there; do not decrease. Also, seek the peace and prosperity of the city to which I have carried you into exile. Pray to the L*ORD *for it, because if it prospers, you too will prosper."*

*This is what the L*ORD *says: "When seventy years are completed for Babylon, I will come to you and fulfill my gracious promise to bring you back to this place. For I know the plans I have for you," declares the L*ORD*, "plans to prosper you and not to harm you, plans to give you hope and a future. Then you will call upon me and come and pray to me, and I will listen to you. You will seek me and find me when you seek me with all your heart. I will be found by you," declares the L*ORD*, "and will bring you back from captivity. I will gather you from all the nations and places where I have banished you," declares the L*ORD*, "and will bring you back to the place from which I carried you into exile."*

God owns time

It's so hard to look beyond our circumstances. For the Jews in the time of Jeremiah, it seemed impossible. The Babylonians had whisked them from their homes and settled them in enemy territory. Into this depressing scene, God sent Jeremiah, the anguished prophet of judgment. But his message this time was one of hope. In essence, he said, "Though your circumstances look bleak, your confinement will be limited. So settle in and make a home away from home for yourselves. As incredible as it sounds, look for and enjoy the moments of joy, even in this place."

Today, endless darkness may seem to surround you, just as the Israelites experienced. Maybe it is hard to remember the last time you felt comfortable.

Whether or not the darkness is of your own making, and whether or not you can see its end, remember this: God owns time. Though he rarely shares his reasons with us, he knows why he allows the pain to continue. And he also knows the date—the day, the hour and the precise minute—when the agony will end. Not only that, but he also knows what he has in store for us when it's over. And because he's God, his plans are always good.

Woe to that wreath, the pride of
*   Ephraim's drunkards,*
to the fading flower, his
*   glorious beauty,*
set on the head of a fertile valley—
to that city, the pride of
*   those laid low by wine!*

See, the Lord *has one who is*
*   powerful and strong.*
Like a hailstorm and a
*   destructive wind,*
like a driving rain and a
*   flooding downpour,*
he will throw it forcefully to
*   the ground.*

That wreath, the pride of
*   Ephraim's drunkards,*
will be trampled underfoot.

That fading flower, his
*   glorious beauty,*
set on the head of a fertile valley,
will be like a fig ripe before harvest—
as soon as someone sees it and
*   takes it in his hand,*
he swallows it.

In that day the Lord *Almighty*
will be a glorious crown,
a beautiful wreath
for the remnant of his people.

Crowned with hope

E phraim, the northern kingdom of Israel, was facing a dismal future as it slid into idolatry. Its wreath of glory was fading fast. Amid Isaiah's prophecy of doom, however, there was a gleam of hope. God had a remnant of faithful people, and God promised to encircle their lives with a glorious crown of strength and hope.

We all can sympathize with the feeling of being trapped in dismal or destructive situations. Perhaps you work with people who see nothing wrong with dishonesty, and you're waging what feels like a losing battle for the truth. Maybe your husband does nothing but discourage and criticize, and you feel yourself fading daily beneath the weight of his words. To those hoping in the darkness, God promises to adorn us with his glory, to encircle our bowed and tired heads with a magnificent wreath: his presence.

God has a special place in his heart for the downtrodden. In reality, we're all beaten back by the world at some point in our day or week. When you feel discouraged or oppressed, picture God's presence, like a lovely wreath, resting on you and strengthening you. Then stand out like a beacon that shines in a world badly in need of hope.

45

David's place was empty again. Then Saul said to his son Jonathan, "Why hasn't the son of Jesse come to the meal, either yesterday or today?" Jonathan answered, "David earnestly asked me for permission to go to Bethlehem. That is why he has not come to the king's table."

Saul's anger flared up at Jonathan and he said to him, "Don't I know that you have sided with the son of Jesse to your own shame and to the shame of the mother who bore you? As long as the son of Jesse lives on this earth, neither you nor your kingdom will be established. Now send and bring him to me, for he must die!" "Why should he be put to death? What has he done?" Jonathan asked his father. But Saul hurled his spear at him to kill him. Then Jonathan knew that his father intended to kill David.

In the morning Jonathan went out to the field for his meeting with David. He had a small boy with him, and he said to the boy, "Run and find the arrows I shoot." As the boy ran, he shot an arrow beyond him. When the boy came to the place where Jonathan's arrow had fallen, Jonathan called out after him, "Isn't the arrow beyond you?" Then he shouted, "Hurry! Go quickly! Don't stop!" The boy picked up the arrow and returned to his master. (The boy knew nothing of all this; only Jonathan and David knew.) Then Jonathan gave his weapons to the boy and said, "Go, carry them back to town."

After the boy had gone, David got up from the south side of the stone and bowed down before Jonathan three times, with his face to the ground. Then they kissed each other and wept together—but David wept the most.

Friends

David and Jonathan made a covenant of friendship. When Samuel anointed David to succeed Jonathan's father as king, Saul erupted in unbridled anger and forced David from the land. But Jonathan swore loyalty to God's chosen heir to the throne.

David and Jonathan's deep friendship was based not on family ties or warm, fuzzy feelings; they were bound by dedication to God and steadfast commitment to one another. Rather than being jealous of David for usurping his potential place as king, Jonathan accepted God's plan to make David king, sacrificially stepping down and supporting his friend. And David reciprocated by remaining loyal to Jonathan and Jonathan's family. Even after Jonathan's death, David kept his vow of loyalty to his dear friend.

In our culture, it seems more common to hear of women who have close friendships than men who do, so we're surprised that one of the most beautiful portraits of friendship in Scripture is the bond between these two warriors, who we might be inclined to think of as unemotional and detached. But we, as women, can model David and Jonathan's friendship. When our friendships are based on our common love for God and our desire for God's best for each other, then our friendships can be as tough and true and deep as the one between David and Jonathan.

Psalm 136:1-9

Give thanks to the Lord, for he is good. His love endures forever.

Give thanks to the God of gods. His love endures forever.

Give thanks to the Lord of lords: His love endures forever.

To him who alone does great wonders, His love endures forever.

Who by his understanding made the heavens, His love endures forever.

Who spread out the earth upon the waters, His love endures forever.

Who made the great lights—His love endures forever.

The sun to govern the day, His love endures forever.

The moon and stars to govern the night; His love endures forever.

Enduring, endearing love

Human love is not flawless. So, where can you find flawless and eternal love? Psalm 136 asserts repeatedly that God's love "endures forever." This antiphonal song served as an anthem or pledge of mutual love between God and his people. Old Testament priests sang the first phrase in these verses while the congregation answered with the refrain: "His love endures forever."

God desires the closeness of such a relationship with each of us for eternity. And his love lasts beyond a lifetime. Not only does God offer us enduring love, he also extends to us endearing love, a strong affection that lifts one higher or increases the value of the one beloved. Enduring speaks of the quantity of God's love, while endearing portrays the quality.

We are nothing. But God loved us before we were lovely. We are his diamonds in the rough. In the rough, a diamond looks like a common pebble. The stone must undergo a finishing process to bring out its full radiance. Many meticulous hours are spent perfecting it.

Like the nation of Israel, God has lifted you out of the rubble of a worthless life. He is polishing and chiseling you into a jewel of great beauty. You are his diamond. You are like a bride being prepared for the bridegroom. And his love endures forever.

"I too was convinced that I ought to do all that was possible to oppose the name of Jesus of Nazareth. I put many of the saints in prison, and when they were put to death, I cast my vote against them. Many a time I went from one synagogue to another to have them punished, and I tried to force them to blaspheme. In my obsession against them, I even went to foreign cities to persecute them.

"On one of these journeys I saw a light from heaven, brighter than the sun, blazing around me and my companions. We all fell to the ground, and I heard a voice saying to me, 'Saul, Saul, why do you persecute me? It is hard for you to kick against the goads.'

"Then I asked, 'Who are you, Lord?'

'I am Jesus, whom you are persecuting,' the Lord replied. 'Now get up and stand on your feet. I have appeared to you to appoint you as a servant and as a witness of what you have seen of me and what I will show you. I will rescue you from your own people and from the Gentiles. I am sending you to them to open their eyes and turn them from darkness to light, and from the power of Satan to God.'

"So then, King Agrippa, I was not disobedient to the vision from heaven. First to those in Damascus, then to those in Jerusalem and in all Judea, and to the Gentiles also, I preached that they should repent and turn to God and prove their repentance by their deeds."

The King and I

Paul's audience before King Agrippa defied protocol. He wore chains rather than formal attire, and he stretched out his hands rather than bowing his head. Paul didn't choose to talk about the weather or share a witty anecdote as if he were meeting royalty. Paul gave his testimony because he understood that telling a personal story could persuade both people and monarchs to follow Christ. His conversion story included three elements common to the stories of all who claim Christ as king.

1. Encountering Christ in the present: Paul, breathing murderous threats, had bullied the disciples throughout Judea. But one day the light of Jesus' presence stopped him dead in his tracks. From then on, Paul called Jesus "Lord" instead of "liar".

2. Repenting of past sin: Paul confessed that he'd done many things in opposition to the name of Jesus, specifically, persecuting the church. Jesus took this personally, saying, "I am Jesus whom you are persecuting." On that day Paul's evil crusade ended when he turned from his sin and turned to Christ.

3. Witnessing to others in the future: Paul was obedient to "the vision from heaven," declaring the gospel in Jerusalem, Judea and then to the Gentiles. Because of Paul's obedience, the world heard Christ's message and was never to be the same.

1 Samuel 30:3-8; 17-19

When David and his men came to Ziklag, they found it destroyed by fire and their wives and sons and daughters taken captive. So David and his men wept aloud until they had no strength left to weep. David's two wives had been captured—Ahinoam of Jezreel and Abigail, the widow of Nabal of Carmel. David was greatly distressed because the men were talking of stoning him; each one was bitter in spirit because of his sons and daughters. But David found strength in the LORD his God.

Then David said to Abiathar the priest, the son of Ahimelech, "Bring me the ephod." Abiathar brought it to him, and David inquired of the LORD, "Shall I pursue this raiding party? Will I overtake them?"

"Pursue them," he answered. "You will certainly overtake them and succeed in the rescue."

David fought them from dusk until the evening of the next day, and none of them got away, except four hundred young men who rode off on camels and fled. David recovered everything the Amalekites had taken, including his two wives. Nothing was missing: young or old, boy or girl, plunder or anything else they had taken. David brought everything back.

Loving in the hard times

One marriage vow many of us take is to stay together "for better or for worse." Still, we go into marriage counting on the "better." But the truth is that nearly every couple faces their own version of the "worse" sooner or later.

David's experience at Ziklag offers us hope in such times. David and his men returned from battle to find their homes destroyed and their families stolen. In the face of this tragedy, these men had a choice to make. All of them, apart from David, chose to stay mired in their misery. But for David this terrible turn of events served as a reminder that in God there always is hope.

Jim is a special education teacher who works primarily with students who have behavioral and emotional problems. His first year of teaching was the most difficult year he and his wife had as a couple. Each day Jim came home emotionally and physically spent. Needless to say, it was a difficult time for his wife as well.

What saved them as a couple was to place their relationship above the other priorities in their lives. Laying that groundwork gave them the firm footing they needed. David, too, had a firm foundation from which to face his trials—he instinctively turned to God.

Psalm 112: 1-7

Praise the LORD.

Blessed is the man who fears the LORD,
who finds great delight in his commands.

His children will be mighty in the land;
the generation of the upright will be blessed.

Wealth and riches are in his house,
and his righteousness endures forever.

Even in darkness light dawns for the upright,
for the gracious and compassionate and righteous man.

Good will come to him who is generous and lends freely,
who conducts his affairs with justice.

Surely he will never be shaken;
a righteous man will be remembered forever.

He will have no fear of bad news;
his heart is steadfast, trusting in the LORD.

A checklist of delight

ow long has it been since you listed the good things God has given you? He created a beautiful world full of all you need: air, water, thousands of varieties of food and much more. In giving you your family, your ability to smell and your sense of humor, God has given you precious gifts.

The psalms give many examples of praise and list many good reasons for thanksgiving. Give thanks in all circumstances? Check. Even in the midst of trials, praise is appropriate because God is keeping track of your enemies while you sleep. Give praise for dark times? Check. Even in darkness his light dawns. Thank him for family? Check. God will meet your needs and watch over your children. Delight in God's commands? Check. Even God's commands are counted among his gracious blessings, for they bring us life.

Have you thanked God for gravity lately? For clouds that shade you from the summer sun, provide the rain and glow at sunrise? For your ears, your nose, your eyes? For giving humankind the ability to create penicillin, the electric light, the telephone, the means of preserving food? For loving you enough to claim you as his child?

Make your own checklist. He is worthy of your praise.

Ecclesiastes 7:10-14

Do not say, "Why were the old days better than these?"
For it is not wise to ask such questions.

Wisdom, like an inheritance, is a good thing
and benefits those who see the sun.

Wisdom is a shelter
as money is a shelter,
but the advantage of knowledge is this:
that wisdom preserves the life of its possessor.

Consider what God has done:
Who can straighten
what he has made crooked?

When times are good, be happy;
but when times are bad, consider:
God has made the one
as well as the other.

Therefore, a man cannot discover
anything about his future.

Remember the good old days?

It's easy to think the past was better than today. Most of us have selective memories. We only remember what we want to remember. You could make the case that it's good to forget the bad. However, when we look at the past through rose-colored glasses, we run the risk of being ungrateful for what we have right now.

Our days, months and years are made up of both good times and bad. The tapestry of life's events makes up the very essence of who we are. Think about today and the difficulties you are encountering: The laundry is piling up. The roof needs fixing. Your kids aren't listening to you. Now consider some of the memories you're making today: Your baby took his first steps. Your daughter graduated from kindergarten, high school or college. You got that big promotion.

Thank God for all your wonderful memories. Take the difficult things to God in prayer. God doesn't waste any of our experiences. He can use the good old days, as well as the not-so-great days, to benefit us, if we let him. The key is to remember things as they really were, to be content with things as they really are and to trust God to take care of the future.

Psalm 51:1-4

Have mercy on me, O God,
according to your unfailing love;
according to your great compassion
blot out my transgressions.

Wash away all my iniquity
and cleanse me from my sin.

For I know my transgressions,
and my sin is always before me.

Against you, you only, have I sinned
and done what is evil in your sight,
so that you are proved right when you speak
and justified when you judge.

Oh God, have mercy

We excuse ourselves so easily. I was tired. He started it. That's the way I was raised. Everyone else does it. It's his fault. It's her fault. Maybe it's even God's fault. But surely it's not my fault! Oh, God, have mercy.

Until we stop making excuses, we aren't ready to be forgiven. Whether we think we are above the law or that our action is okay if others started it, our excuses cover us as poorly as Adam and Eve's fig leaves in the Garden of Eden. Sometimes we change the name to cover our sin: It's not gossip; it's sharing. It's not coveting; it's admiring. It's not lying; it's explaining. Oh, God, have mercy.

God doesn't forgive excuses. But God does forgive sin. He's waiting for us to call it what he calls it: sin. When we acknowledge our sin and repent, God removes sin as far as the east is from the west.

When the prophet Nathan confronted King David about his sin, David's repentance was deep and real. In Psalm 51 he put his feelings into words. He cried out for God's mercy, asking God to cleanse him of his sin, to teach him wisdom and to heal his conscience and his emotions.

God did extraordinary miracles through Paul, so that even handkerchiefs and aprons that had touched him were taken to the sick, and their illnesses were cured and the evil spirits left them.

Some Jews who went around driving out evil spirits tried to invoke the name of the Lord Jesus over those who were demon-possessed. They would say, "In the name of Jesus, whom Paul preaches, I command you to come out." Seven sons of Sceva, a Jewish chief priest, were doing this. (One day) the evil spirit answered them, "Jesus I know, and I know about Paul, but who are you?" Then the man who had the evil spirit jumped on them and overpowered them all. He gave them such a beating that they ran out of the house naked and bleeding.

When this became known to the Jews and Greeks living in Ephesus, they were all seized with fear, and the name of the Lord Jesus was held in high honor. Many of those who believed now came and openly confessed their evil deeds. A number who had practiced sorcery brought their scrolls together and burned them publicly. When they calculated the value of the scrolls, the total came to fifty thousand drachmas. In this way the word of the Lord spread widely and grew in power.

Name-droppers

Name-droppers are known for annoying those who overhear their outrageous claims. Casually sprinkling their conversations with the names of famous people, they aim to impress their listeners. Some imply a familiarity with illustrious people, as if they are on a first-name basis.

In Acts 19, we meet the seven sons of Sceva, who employed name-dropping in their profession as exorcists. They incorporated the name of Jesus into their effort to drive out demons. But it backfired. If the disciples were able to cast out demons in Jesus' name, why couldn't the sons of Sceva? It was largely because they profaned God's name by taking it in vain. They knew the name of the Lord, but not the Lord of the name.

The sons of Sceva presumptuously took Christ's name in vain, but there are other ways to take his name in vain: repeating the Lord's name as a part of rote or routine, professing to be a Christian without obeying God's commands, or praising God with the lips but not from the heart.

There is power in God's name, but we can learn from this story to be careful not to drop God's name unless we have a relationship with him. When we honor the Lord's name, we are honoring our Lord.

Some time later the brook dried up because there had been no rain in the land. Then the word of the Lord came to him: "Go at once to Zarephath of Sidon and stay there. I have commanded a widow in that place to supply you with food." So he went to Zarephath. When he came to the town gate, a widow was there gathering sticks. He called to her and asked, "Would you bring me a little water in a jar so I may have a drink?" As she was going to get it, he called, "And bring me, please, a piece of bread."

"As surely as the Lord your God lives," she replied, "I don't have any bread—only a handful of flour in a jar and a little oil in a jug. I am gathering a few sticks to take home and make a meal for myself and my son, that we may eat it—and die."

Elijah said to her, "Don't be afraid. Go home and do as you have said. But first make a small cake of bread for me from what you have and bring it to me, and then make something for yourself and your son. For this is what the Lord the God of Israel, says: 'The jar of flour will not be used up and the jug of oil will not run dry until the day the Lord gives rain on the land.' "

She went away and did as Elijah had told her. So there was food every day for Elijah and for the woman and her family. For the jar of flour was not used up and the jug of oil did not run dry, in keeping with the word of the Lord spoken by Elijah.

Nothing's impossible

"Faith sees the invisible, believes the unbelievable and receives the impossible." It may be easy to say these words when times are good and food is plentiful. But these words were spoken by Corrie ten Boom, who, along with her sister Betsie, suffered horribly at the hands of Nazi guards at the Ravensbruck concentration camp.

Corrie tried to hoard a tiny brown bottle of liquid vitamins. She wanted to save the small amount left for the weakest inmates. Amazingly, every time Corrie tilted the bottle for a sick inmate, one drop would pour out. When there couldn't possibly be any more, another dose was dispensed.

Elijah was not in a prison camp, but the land was suffering from God's judgment of drought and famine. When he was hiding from King Ahab and he found refuge with a widow and her son, their jar of flour and oil never ran dry.

It may seem impossible to you that God would supply you with such basic things as flour and vitamins, but these stories are about the Savior who is the same yesterday, today and forever. Ask God to provide everything you need to live. He will multiply his grace toward you in your times of trouble. Believe it. All things are possible with God.

Jeremiah 44:15-22

Then all the men who knew that their wives were burning incense to other gods, along with all the women who were present—a large assembly—and all the people living in Lower and Upper Egypt, said to Jeremiah, "We will not listen to the message you have spoken to us in the name of the LORD! We will certainly do everything we said we would: We will burn incense to the Queen of Heaven and will pour out drink offerings to her just as we and our fathers, our kings and our officials did in the towns of Judah and in the streets of Jerusalem. At that time we had plenty of food and were well off and suffered no harm. But ever since we stopped burning incense to the Queen of Heaven and pouring out drink offerings to her, we have had nothing and have been perishing by sword and famine."

The women added, "When we burned incense to the Queen of Heaven and poured out drink offerings to her, did not our husbands know that we were making cakes like her image and pouring out drink offerings to her?"

Then Jeremiah said to all the people, both men and women, who were answering him, "Did not the LORD remember and think about the incense burned in the towns of Judah and the streets of Jerusalem by you and your fathers, your kings and your officials and the people of the land? When the LORD could no longer endure your wicked actions and the detestable things you did, your land became an object of cursing and a desolate waste without inhabitants, as it is today."

No more blame game

The blame game has been going on for a long time. During King Manasseh's reign in Israel, husbands and wives enjoyed prosperity. But by the time of King Josiah, those benefits had disappeared. People wanted the good times to return. Instead of appealing to the God of Israel, however, the people placed their trust in other gods.

Yet when the prophet Jeremiah berated the Jews who had fled to Egypt after the fall of Jerusalem for their faithlessness to the Lord, the women danced away from responsibility, passing it off on their husbands. The men played the blame game, too, blaming the God of Israel for not taking care of them. But Jeremiah didn't let anyone off the hook. He held both men and women responsible for worshiping false gods.

Similarly, in marriage we are responsible for our actions, both individually and as a couple. The one who sins is primarily responsible for that sin. But because we are in a covenant relationship we also have the responsibility to help each other live right before God. Without being overly self-righteous or condemning, we need to understand the full extent of each other's sin, forgive what can be forgiven, work to loosen the grip of that sin, and hold each other accountable.

1 Samuel 3:2-10

One night Eli, whose eyes were becoming so weak that he could barely see, was lying down in his usual place. The lamp of God had not yet gone out, and Samuel was lying down in the temple of the Lord, where the ark of God was. Then the Lord called Samuel. Samuel answered, "Here I am." And he ran to Eli and said, "Here I am; you called me." But Eli said, "I did not call; go back and lie down." So he went and lay down. Again the Lord called, "Samuel!" And Samuel got up and went to Eli and said, "Here I am; you called me." "My son," Eli said, "I did not call; go back and lie down."

Now Samuel did not yet know the Lord: The word of the Lord had not yet been revealed to him.

The Lord called Samuel a third time, and Samuel got up and went to Eli and said, "Here I am; you called me."

Then Eli realized that the Lord was calling the boy. So Eli told Samuel, "Go and lie down, and if he calls you, say, 'Speak, Lord, for your servant is listening.' " So Samuel went and lay down in his place.

The Lord came and stood there, calling as at the other times, "Samuel! Samuel!" Then Samuel said, "Speak, for your servant is listening."

Are you listening?

When was the last time you heard from God? The adolescent boy Samuel was lying in the temple. It was still night. He was probably lonely, having been separated from his family and dedicated by his mother Hannah to work for the old, blind priest Eli in the temple.

As Samuel drowsed, the sound of his name cut through the dimness. Naturally, Samuel thought Eli had called. "Here I am," replied the boy. Again, "Samuel!" Samuel listened keenly, but the summons didn't come from Eli. God himself called Samuel, and Eli had taught the boy the right response: "Speak, for your servant is listening."

What made Samuel so ready to hear God's voice? For one thing, he was a faithful and obedient servant. He was ready to respond to his master, and his willingness made him ready to respond to God as well. Samuel was also in the right place to listen. Are you?

If you want to hear God speak, do what you can to be ready. Be prepared when you're in a silent place. Seek an inner silence as well. When God calls you, respond: "Speak, Lord, for your servant is listening."

Psalm 89:1-4; 49

I will sing of the LORD's great love forever;
with my mouth I will make your faithfulness known through all generations.

I will declare that your love stands firm forever,
that you established your faithfulness in heaven itself.

You said, "I have made a covenant with my chosen one,
I have sworn to David my servant,

'I will establish your line forever
and make your throne firm through all generations.' "

O Lord, where is your former great love,
which in your faithfulness you swore to David?

Holding out hope

We can't be sure of the identity of Ethan the Ezrahite, the ascribed author of Psalm 89. But at any rate, the psalmist was depressed and mystified when he asked, "Lord, where is your former great love, which in your faithfulness you swore to David?" (Verse 49).

Ethan's psalm resonates with some of us with regard to our marriages. Every couple that celebrates a wedding echoes the enthusiasm of the first four verses: God's love endures forever. But too many relationships run into hard times. After one couple struggled through years of infidelity, they finally decided to call it quits but were unsure of what to do. They put parting on hold and during that time they fell in love all over again.

Some years later they had a 25th anniversary celebration. When the couple stood to thank the large gathering of friends for coming, the tears flowed. Then they revealed why all of the guests had been invited. Each of them, they said, had kept faith in God for them even while they lost courage and confidence. They had tried, failed, prayed and grown bitter. But they had wrestled with God on the couple's behalf, using both praise and lament, similar to the way Ethan had in Psalm 89.

2 Samuel 6:12-19

So David went down and brought up the ark of God from the house of Obed-Edom to the City of David with rejoicing. When those who were carrying the ark of the Lord had taken six steps, he sacrificed a bull and a fattened calf. David, wearing a linen ephod, danced before the Lord with all his might, while he and the entire house of Israel brought up the ark of the Lord with shouts and the sound of trumpets.

As the ark of the Lord was entering the City of David, Michal daughter of Saul watched from a window. And when she saw King David leaping and dancing before the Lord, she despised him in her heart.

They brought the ark of the Lord and set it in its place inside the tent that David had pitched for it, and David sacrificed burnt offerings and fellowship offerings before the Lord. After he had finished sacrificing the burnt offerings and fellowship offerings, he blessed the people in the name of the Lord Almighty. Then he gave a loaf of bread, a cake of dates and a cake of raisins to each person in the whole crowd of Israelites, both men and women. And all the people went to their homes.

Celebrate!

I f we could have seen King David bringing the ark of the covenant back to Jerusalem we might have been shocked that he and other dignitaries came into the city leaping, shouting and dancing through the streets. At least one person was more than shocked; she was angry. Michal, David's wife, "despised him in her heart." But David didn't care what others thought, even if the disapproval came from one of his wives.

David rejoiced because the ark of the covenant, Israel's most sacred object of worship, had been reclaimed from the Philistines. David had every reason to dance for joy.

We all celebrate births and birthdays, weddings and anniversaries, graduations, promotions, holidays and winning seasons. But do we ever, like King David, celebrate God's blessings without concern for what others may think?

We don't have to shake tambourines to exhibit hearts of worship. Our rejoicing may be outwardly exuberant or quietly subdued. But when our hearts are filled with gratitude, outward expressions of praise will naturally overflow. As women of God, we have every reason to dance with joy that the Lord is among us. If we choose to raise our hands or bend our knees in true worship, it's not undignified; it's a genuine expression of praise.

The LORD said to Moses: "When a person commits a violation and sins unintentionally in regard to any of the LORD's holy things, he is to bring to the LORD as a penalty a ram from the flock, one without defect and of the proper value in silver, according to the sanctuary shekel. It is a guilt offering. He must make restitution for what he has failed to do in regard to the holy things, add a fifth of the value to that and give it all to the priest, who will make atonement for him with the ram as a guilt offering, and he will be forgiven.

"If a person sins and does what is forbidden in any of the LORD's commands, even though he does not know it, he is guilty and will be held responsible. He is to bring to the priest as a guilt offering a ram from the flock, one without defect and of the proper value. In this way the priest will make atonement for him for the wrong he has committed unintentionally, and he will be forgiven. It is a guilt offering; he has been guilty of wrongdoing against the LORD."

Not guilty

I sn't it painful to harm others intentionally? Premeditated evils can be set right by our finite sense of justice, even if guilt then rests on our own head. But imagine the fear and frustration of being held accountable for hundreds of violations that you committed without knowing. In Old Testament times, you would certainly have been guilty of such unwitting sins, and they would have required blood sacrifice. The Law of God was clear: no one could be good enough.

The sacrifices of the Old Testament foreshadowed the ultimate sacrifice: Jesus Christ. When Jesus offered himself on the cross, he paid the debt of sin in full. He declared his followers "not guilty."

Women today are often burdened by guilt. We are inundated with "shoulds" and "oughts." We feel guilty if we work; guilty if we don't; guilty for not spending enough time with our husbands, kids and friends; and guilty for not taking time for God and ourselves. We have a hard time knowing when we are really guilty and when we suffer from false guilt. But Jesus' declaration from the cross that we are not guilty covers all of our sins—even the unintentional ones. Instead of blood sacrifice, we can make offerings of gratitude: repentance, praise and service.

Jesus left the synagogue and went to the home of Simon. Now Simon's mother-in-law was suffering from a high fever, and they asked Jesus to help her. So he bent over her and rebuked the fever, and it left her. She got up at once and began to wait on them.

When the sun was setting, the people brought to Jesus all who had various kinds of sickness, and laying his hands on each one, he healed them. Moreover, demons came out of many people, shouting, "You are the Son of God!" But he rebuked them and would not allow them to speak, because they knew he was the Christ.

At daybreak Jesus went out to a solitary place. The people were looking for him and when they came to where he was, they tried to keep him from leaving them. But he said, "I must preach the good news of the kingdom of God to the other towns also, because that is why I was sent." And he kept on preaching in the synagogues of Judea.

From suffering to serving

L uke tells us that Simon's mother-in-law was sick with a high fever. This was no ordinary cold. She was really, really sick and suffering. But the disciples didn't run to the local apothecary; they asked Jesus to help her.

The Great Physician bent over the tired woman's body and told the fever to leave—and it left! And amazingly, she didn't need rest to recover from her ordeal. She was so completely healed that "she got up at once and began to wait on them."

She probably could have stayed on her sickbed for a few days, let other people wait on her, gotten a little more sympathy and emotional mileage out of that fever, and no one would have known (except Jesus). But some women have a gift of serving others, no matter what.

You might be one of those women. You think, "I don't have time to rest, and I really don't have time to be sick." But let's face it, sometimes we get sick—or just sick and tired. That's when we can ask for help from the One who is the source of healing and strength. There's nothing wrong with finding a healthy balance between meeting your own needs and meeting the needs of others.

Job 13:1-4, 14-15

"My eyes have seen all this,
my ears have heard and understood it.

What you know, I also know;
I am not inferior to you.

But I desire to speak to the Almighty
and to argue my case with God.

You, however, smear me with lies;
you are worthless physicians, all of you!

Why do I put myself in jeopardy
and take my life in my hands?

Though he slay me, yet will I hope in him;
I will surely defend my ways to his face."

The patience of Job

Even well-intentioned people, like Job's foolish counselors, believe that all suffering or sickness is the direct result of sin. Job's friends tried to convince him that he had done something to displease God, that somehow Job was responsible for the horrible things that had happened to him. But this could not be farther from the truth. For some reason, God chose to use Job as an example of patience in the midst of great suffering.

When something tragic happens, we often scramble to figure out why. Did I sin? Did they sin? If we didn't sin, then who did? Like Job's friends, we just want to affix blame so we can make some kind of sense out of the seemingly senseless. But not all suffering is the direct result of sin.

The simple truth is that God is not constrained to tell us why bad things happen to us. But he will let us know how to walk through them with patience and hope. Yes, Job had some questions he wanted God to answer. But despite his questions Job could still faithfully proclaim, "Though he slay me, yet will I hope in him." Can the same be said of you?

Psalm 100:1-5

Shout for joy to the LORD, all the earth.

Worship the LORD with gladness;
come before him with joyful songs.

Know that the LORD is God.
It is he who made us, and we are his;
we are his people, the sheep of his pasture.

Enter his gates with thanksgiving
and his courts with praise;
give thanks to him and praise his name.

For the LORD is good and his love endures forever;
his faithfulness continues through all generations.

The wow in worship

Sometimes we lack the wow in our worship. Psalm 100 offers us a spiritual pick-me-up. It reveals that the more you know about God's nature, the more you'll express your love for him. Information leads to adoration. When the psalmist reflected on the Lord as God, Creator and Shepherd, it resulted in worship, gladness and joyful songs. It's true that to know him is to love him.

Knowing that the Lord is God identifies him as the only true God. He exists before all, after all and above all. He possesses unlimited power, unfathomable knowledge and an unavoidable presence. God is big!

A little girl listened as her father read family devotions. She seemed awed by her parents' talk of God's limitless power. "Daddy," she asked, "how big is God?" Her father answered, "Honey, he is always a lot bigger than what you need."

Believing that God is bigger than your situation produces passion in your praise. Showing gratitude to your Shepherd can produce gladness in your heart. Understanding that the Lord is bigger than any of your needs, that he is your Creator—that you belong to him—can't help but put the wow back into your worship!

Jesus said to his disciples: "Things that cause people to sin are bound to come, but woe to that person through whom they come. It would be better for him to be thrown into the sea with a millstone tied around his neck than for him to cause one of these little ones to sin. So watch yourselves. If your brother sins, rebuke him, and if he repents, forgive him. If he sins against you seven times in a day, and seven times comes back to you and says, 'I repent,' forgive him."

The apostles said to the Lord, "Increase our faith!"

He replied, "If you have faith as small as a mustard seed, you can say to this mulberry tree, 'Be uprooted and planted in the sea,' and it will obey you.

"Suppose one of you had a servant plowing or looking after the sheep. Would he say to the servant when he comes in from the field, 'Come along now and sit down to eat'? Would he not rather say, 'Prepare my supper, get yourself ready and wait on me while I eat and drink; after that you may eat and drink'? Would he thank the servant because he did what he was told to do? So you also, when you have done everything you were told to do, should say, 'We are unworthy servants; we have only done our duty.' "

Giving forgiveness a chance

In Luke Jesus tells us over and over again to forgive. Is he instructing us to be doormats and let others run over us? Or does he know something about forgiveness that will free us? As we ponder our attitude toward forgiveness, we might say, "Easier than done." A husband and wife can inflict pain on each other that scars their relationship for the rest of their lives. At the very least, a spouse can perpetuate annoyances and frustrations that make the other spouse blow up.

Jesus is not telling us that we need to condone behavior that hurts us. Nor is he telling us to forgive only those people who ask for forgiveness. And, he is not telling us to ignore repeated sinful behavior in our spouse. After all, repeatedly forgiving wrong without confronting the reasons for it will ultimately kill trust in any relationship.

What Jesus is telling us is that denying forgiveness to the offender will ultimately hurt us more than it hurts them. For when we lug around a load of self-pity and bitterness and an attitude of martyrdom, we put a big roadblock of resentment between ourselves and the people who have hurt us. A future relationship with someone we refuse to forgive may become lost forever.

At that time King Xerxes reigned from his royal throne in the citadel of Susa, and in the third year of his reign he gave a banquet for all his nobles and officials. The military leaders of Persia and Media, the princes, and the nobles of the provinces were present.

For a full 180 days he displayed the vast wealth of his kingdom and the splendor and glory of his majesty. When these days were over, the king gave a banquet, lasting seven days, in the enclosed garden of the king's palace, for all the people from the least to the greatest, who were in the citadel of Susa. The garden had hangings of white and blue linen, fastened with cords of white linen and purple material to silver rings on marble pillars. There were couches of gold and silver on a mosaic pavement of porphyry, marble, mother-of-pearl and other costly stones. Wine was served in

goblets of gold, each one different from the other, and the royal wine was abundant, in keeping with the king's liberality. By the king's command each guest was allowed to drink in his own way, for the king instructed all the wine stewards to serve each man what he wished.

Queen Vashti also gave a banquet for the women in the royal palace of King Xerxes.

On the seventh day, when King Xerxes was in high spirits from wine, he commanded the seven eunuchs who served him—Mehuman, Biztha, Harbona, Bigtha, Abagtha, Zethar and Carcas—to bring before him Queen Vashti, wearing her royal crown, in order to display her beauty to the people and nobles, for she was lovely to look at. But when the attendants delivered the king's command, Queen Vashti refused to come. Then the king became furious and burned with anger.

When you have to say no

King Xerxes, the military leader of the Medes and Persians, tried to fulfill his father's failed plan to conquer Greece. Esther 1 records what may have been Xerxes' planning meeting for the military campaigns of 482-479 B.C. During the lengthy meeting the men feasted and drank extensively. At one point Xerxes commanded his wife, Vashti, to appear before the assembled men. We are not told why Vashti refused, but given the circumstances and the rate at which we can assume the men were consuming alcohol, perhaps she was afraid they were asking her to act immodestly, or worse.

Xerxes reacted like a spoiled child. He was furious that his order had not been obeyed. His advisers proposed deposing Vashti as queen and banishing her from the presence of the king. Ultimately, Esther was chosen to be the new queen, placing her in a position to intervene at a time when her people were threatened.

Within this story, Vashti often goes unrecognized as a heroine. Yet perhaps that should be acknowledged, particularly within the context of marriage. For while Vashti had been obedient to her husband in all things, there came a point when she just could not do something she knew was wrong. In our marriages we need mutual submission and respect. But we also need personal courage to say no to one another when decency is twisted or when obedience to little things would deny obedience to God's greater ways.

Genesis 24:34-38, 42-46, 54, 58

So he said, "I am Abraham's servant. The LORD has blessed my master abundantly, and he has become wealthy. My master's wife Sarah has borne him a son in her old age, and he has given him everything he owns. And my master made me swear an oath, and said, 'You must not get a wife for my son from the daughters of the Canaanites, in whose land I live, but go to my father's family and to my own clan, and get a wife for my son.'

"When I came to the spring today, I said, 'O LORD, God of my master Abraham, if you will, please grant success to the journey on which I have come. See, I am standing beside this spring; if a maiden comes out to draw water and I say to her, "Please let me drink a little water from your jar," and if she says to me, "Drink, and I'll draw water for your camels too," let her be the one the LORD has chosen for my master's son.'

"Before I finished praying in my heart, Rebekah came out, with her jar on her shoulder. She went down to the spring and drew water, and I said to her, 'Please give me a drink.' She quickly lowered her jar from her shoulder and said, 'Drink, and I'll water your camels too.' So I drank, and she watered the camels also."

Then he and the men who were with him ate and drank and spent the night there. When they got up the next morning, he said, "Send me on my way to my master."

So they called Rebekah and asked her, "Will you go with this man?" "I will go," she said.

Principles of a good match

The story of Abraham sending his servant to find a wife for his son Isaac illustrates several biblical principles for marriage. The first principle is that prayer is important in all stages and in all decisions regarding marriage. A second principle is that we should marry a person who shares our beliefs. And a third principle is that commitment is crucial.

A marriage was once compared to buying a car. If you know this is the only car you'll ever have, you will take very good care of it. If, on the other hand, you buy the car thinking you can always junk it and get another one, you're less likely to change the oil or pay attention to the warning lights on the dashboard.

While we want to heed the Bible's principles on marriage, we don't have to follow some of its customs such as arranged marriages. In American culture we value individual choice and generally shun match-making, unless it's on the Internet and we control the criteria.

Whether or not you're sure you married the one and only person in the world for you, once the choice is made, all other choices are off the table. So, let God help your marriage become all that it can be.

When the whole nation had finished crossing the Jordan, the LORD said to Joshua, "Choose twelve men from among the people, one from each tribe, and tell them to take up twelve stones from the middle of the Jordan from right where the priests stood and to carry them over with you and put them down at the place where you stay tonight."

So Joshua called together the twelve men he had appointed from the Israelites, one from each tribe, and said to them, "Go over before the ark of the LORD your God into the middle of the Jordan. Each of you is to take up a stone on his shoulder, according to the number of the tribes of the Israelites, to serve as a sign among you. In the future, when your children ask you, 'What do these stones mean?' tell them that the flow of the Jordan was cut off before the ark of the covenant of the LORD. When it crossed the Jordan, the waters of the Jordan were cut off. These stones are to be a memorial to the people of Israel forever."

So the Israelites did as Joshua commanded them.

Memory stone collection

ome couples have a commemorative wedding plate with their wedding date on it hanging in their home. Every time they see the plate, they're reminded of their wedding day.

Reminders of significant events accomplish a variety of purposes. God directed Joshua to set up a pile of stones taken from the Jordan River after the children of Israel crossed the river on dry ground. The stones served as a reminder that God had brought his people into the promised land. The stones also functioned as a device that would encourage the next generation of Israelites to ask their parents what the stones meant.

If you have children, you know that they can ask a multitude of questions. No doubt children in ancient Israel behaved in the same way. The stones from the Jordan River were not artifacts of history, they served as a reminder of God's mighty acts. The pile of stones provided fathers and mothers an opportunity to explain to their children what God had done.

Ezra 8: 21-23, 31-32

There, by the Ahava Canal, I proclaimed a fast, so that we might humble ourselves before our God and ask him for a safe journey for us and our children, with all our possessions. I was ashamed to ask the king for soldiers and horsemen to protect us from enemies on the road, because we had told the king, "The gracious hand of our God is on everyone who looks to him, but his great anger is against all who forsake him." So we fasted and petitioned our God about this, and he answered our prayer.

On the twelfth day of the first month we set out from the Ahava Canal to go to Jerusalem. The hand of our God was on us, and he protected us from enemies and bandits along the way. So we arrived in Jerusalem, where we rested three days.

Total dependence

zra sets a great example for anyone facing an unknown future. Before he and a group of returning exiles began their 900-mile trek back to Jerusalem, they fasted and prayed for a safe journey. They trusted God would guide them. God is also with you to guide you, regardless of your circumstances. Take a step of faith and you'll discover that faith will lead you where reason may not.

Faith and reason have been compared to two travelers. Think of Faith as a woman who can walk twenty or thirty miles at a time without flagging, while Reason is a child who can only muster the strength to go two or three miles. One day Reason said to Faith, "Oh, Faith, let me walk with you." But faith replied, "Oh, Reason, you can never walk with me!" Nevertheless, they set out together. When they came to a deep river, Reason said, "I can never ford this," but Faith waded through it singing. When they reached a high mountain, Reason despaired. But Faith carried Reason on her back. The writer of this old tale said, "Oh, how dependent upon Faith is Reason!"

Why has God made faith the indispensable ingredient in our journey of faith? Perhaps so that we will become totally dependent on him.

Acts 12:5-11

So Peter was kept in prison, but the church was earnestly praying to God for him.

The night before Herod was to bring him to trial, Peter was sleeping between two soldiers, bound with two chains, and sentries stood guard at the entrance. Suddenly an angel of the Lord appeared and a light shone in the cell. He struck Peter on the side and woke him up. "Quick, get up!" he said, and the chains fell off Peter's wrists.

Then the angel said to him, "Put on your clothes and sandals." And Peter did so. "Wrap your cloak around you and follow me," the angel told him. Peter followed him out of the prison, but he had no idea that what the angel was doing was really happening; he thought he was seeing a vision. They passed the first and second guards and came to the iron gate leading to the city. It opened for them by itself, and they went through it. When they had walked the length of one street, suddenly the angel left him.

Then Peter came to himself and said, "Now I know without a doubt that the Lord sent his angel and rescued me from Herod's clutches and from everything the Jewish people were anticipating."

Praying through

Something mysterious takes place when we pray. God doesn't need our prayers, yet he uses them. In the inexplicable workings of heaven and earth, our prayers make a difference.

In this passage in the book of Acts, the believers who had gathered at Mary's house had just witnessed the death of James. They knew that Peter was next in line for Herod's sword, and they knew that they were powerless to do anything about it. But when they prayed to God for Peter, something miraculous happened. An angel stepped into the jail cell, Peter's chains fell off and the locked doors opened. On what might have been Peter's last night alive, God intervened in ways neither Peter nor the praying Christians could fathom.

We can never know how God will answer the prayers of his people. We only know that he tells us to pray about anything and everything. We may feel powerless in ourselves, but when we lift our prayers to God, when we "pray through" our difficulties, the door is opened for God to step in and do the miraculous.

Matthew 1:18-21, 24-25

This is how the birth of Jesus Christ came about: His mother Mary was pledged to be married to Joseph, but before they came together, she was found to be with child through the Holy Spirit. Because Joseph her husband was a righteous man and did not want to expose her to public disgrace, he had in mind to divorce her quietly.

But after he had considered this, an angel of the Lord appeared to him in a dream and said, "Joseph son of David, do not be afraid to take Mary home as your wife, because what is conceived in her is from the Holy Spirit. She will give birth to a son, and you are to give him the name Jesus, because he will save his people from their sins."

When Joseph woke up, he did what the angel of the Lord had commanded him and took Mary home as his wife. But he had no union with her until she gave birth to a son. And he gave him the name Jesus.

Impossible dream

For centuries God's people had been waiting for the promised Messiah, each family hoping he would be born to them. Then in an "impossible" dream, Joseph received a revelation from heaven telling him that Mary, his betrothed, was going to bear God's son. An angel of the Lord instructed Joseph not to shame her, but to marry her and raise the Son of God as his own child.

But was the dream really a nightmare for Joseph? He must have wrestled with all that this news implied. For the rest of his life he might live with the whispers that he hadn't been able to wait until the marriage bed, or, worse, that he was raising another man's child. But Joseph put these doubts and questions aside and decided to accept the charge God had given him regardless of the personal implications. And God blessed him, entrusting him with Jesus, who surely must have been a profound joy to have as a child.

You may have dreamed an impossible dream only to have it turn into a nightmare. If so, do what Joseph did when facing the impossible. Bring Jesus into your home and invite him into your heart. He doesn't know the word impossible because with him all things are possible.

Psalm 113:1-2, 9

Praise the LORD.
Praise, O servants of the LORD,
praise the name of the LORD.

Let the name of the LORD be praised,
both now and forevermore.

He settles the barren woman in her home
as a happy mother of children.
Praise the LORD.

Kids: blessed troubles

When you hold your newborn baby for the first time you forget about the hours you just spent in intense labor. All you know is that God heard your request for a baby and has blessed the two of you with a child of your own. But, next thing you know the baby throws up on your shoulder or refuses to sleep at night!

When you don't have children, parenthood sounds idyllic. You envision babies cooing and preschoolers holding your hand. You imagine your child drawing you pictures, handing you flowers, kissing your nose and giggling at your jokes. Certainly there are such moments, but there are also nights without sleep, hours of tedium and tension, trips to the emergency room and tantrums in the mall.

It's been said that the trouble with children is that when they're not a lump in your throat they're a pain in your neck. In trying times it's tempting to grab your spouse's hand and turn and run. We don't know what we are doing most of the time as parents, but thank God that he does! When it comes to raising children, happiness is knowing that God gives his grace, strength and mercy to those who need it.

While the whole assembly of Israel was standing there, the king turned around and blessed them. Then he said: "Praise be to the LORD, the God of Israel, who with his hands has fulfilled what he promised with his mouth to my father David. For he said, 'Since the day I brought my people out of Egypt, I have not chosen a city in any tribe of Israel to have a temple built for my Name to be there, nor have I chosen anyone to be the leader over my people Israel. But now I have chosen Jerusalem for my Name to be there, and I have chosen David to rule my people Israel.'

"My father David had it in his heart to build a temple for the Name of the LORD, the God of Israel. But the LORD said to my father David, 'Because it was in your heart to build a temple for my Name, you did well to have this in your heart. Nevertheless, you are not the one to build the temple, but your son, who is your own flesh and blood—he is the one who will build the temple for my Name.'

"The LORD has kept the promise he made. I have succeeded David my father and now I sit on the throne of Israel, just as the LORD promised, and I have built the temple for the Name of the LORD, the God of Israel."

Loose ends

We can't always finish what we start. That idea runs counter to our sensibilities as women. Of course we have to finish. But sometimes we're supposed to leave some loose ends dangling.

King David knew a thing or two about loose ends. He had the noble ambition of building a temple for God. But God had in mind a different man for the job, David's son Solomon. When Solomon became king he picked up the loose ends his father had left and went to work. The plans were David's but the work of constructing the temple belonged to King Solomon. If David had pressed ahead with constructing the temple, not only would he have been disobedient, but he also would have deprived his son of a unique opportunity to use his wisdom, gifts and talents to serve God.

Is there a task or position you are clinging to that God is asking you to release? The simple truth is that loose ends leave room for someone else to come along and continue the work in new and unique ways. And God may want you to move forward to a different phase of life. Leaving room for loose ends allows God's kingdom to extend beyond our influence and reach into eternity.

After Saul returned from pursuing the Philistines, he was told, "David is in the Desert of En Gedi." So Saul took three thousand chosen men from all Israel and set out to look for David and his men near the Crags of the Wild Goats.

He came to the sheep pens along the way; a cave was there, and Saul went in to relieve himself. David and his men were far back in the cave. The men said, "This is the day the LORD spoke of when he said to you, 'I will give your enemy into your hands for you to deal with as you wish.' " Then David crept up unnoticed and cut off a corner of Saul's robe.

Afterward, David was conscience-stricken for having cut off a corner of his robe. He said to his men, "The LORD forbid that I should do such a thing to my master, the LORD's anointed, or lift my hand against him; for he is the anointed of the LORD." With these words David rebuked his men and did not allow them to attack Saul. And Saul left the cave and went his way.

Being misunderstood

We've all been misunderstood or mistreated. No matter how hard we work at doing things right, there may be someone who doesn't see things the way we do or like the way we do things. But you can choose to forget the insults and wrong.

David seemed to live by this philosophy. He didn't deserve to be persecuted by King Saul. He had served the king well. Yet here we find the two men at odds in a desert oasis, meeting unexpectedly in the back of a cold, damp cave. With a single, well-placed thrust of his sword, David could have killed Saul. But he recognized that Saul was God's anointed, so David chose to forget Saul's wrongs and not lay a hand against him.

How do you respond when you've been misunderstood? Can you leave matters in God's hands and choose to forget? Can you be content to wait for God to set things right, on his timetable rather than yours? The next time you feel misunderstood or mistreated, remember that you're following in some pretty big footsteps. King David was persecuted for doing God's bidding and did not retaliate when he was attacked. What will you do the next time you're wronged?

2 Corinthians 1:3-11

Praise be to the God and Father of our Lord Jesus Christ, the Father of compassion and the God of all comfort, who comforts us in all our troubles, so that we can comfort those in any trouble with the comfort we ourselves have received from God. For just as the sufferings of Christ flow over into our lives, so also through Christ our comfort overflows. If we are distressed, it is for your comfort and salvation; if we are comforted, it is for your comfort, which produces in you patient endurance of the same sufferings we suffer. And our hope for you is firm, because we know that just as you share in our sufferings, so also you share in our comfort.

We do not want you to be uninformed, brothers, about the hardships we suffered in the province of Asia. We were under great pressure, far beyond our ability to endure, so that we despaired even of life. Indeed, in our hearts we felt the sentence of death. But this happened that we might not rely on ourselves but on God, who raises the dead. He has delivered us from such a deadly peril, and he will deliver us. On him we have set our hope that he will continue to deliver us, as you help us by your prayers. Then many will give thanks on our behalf for the gracious favor granted us in answer to the prayers of many.

Opening up to others

How do you define a good marriage? Most of us would answer by talking about how the relationship affects the people in it. But when you really think about it, a good marriage isn't just good for the couple and the family they create; it is good for everyone who gets drawn into its orbit.

Paul's letter to the Corinthians was written to a community, not an individual. In it Paul was offering a vision of what the church could be if people looked beyond their individual needs and started thinking of other people. His hope was that believers would share the love and compassion God had given them with everyone they met. Paul wanted believers to expand their vision and avoid letting interpersonal issues get in the way of reaching out to others.

Naturally, developing a marriage that benefits others means making sure that the marriage benefits the couple as well. Married couples can enhance their relationship by sharing the comfort, love and compassion they've been given. The shared purpose of such a marriage mission bonds a couple like nothing else. Really, what could be better than bringing about the kingdom of God with your best friends?

Exodus 16:2-8

In the desert the whole community grumbled against Moses and Aaron. The Israelites said to them, "If only we had died by the LORD's hand in Egypt! There we sat around pots of meat and ate all the food we wanted, but you have brought us out into this desert to starve this entire assembly to death."

Then the LORD said to Moses, "I will rain down bread from heaven for you. The people are to go out each day and gather enough for that day. In this way I will test them and see whether they will follow my instructions. On the sixth day they are to prepare what they bring in, and that is to be twice as much as they gather on the other days."

So Moses and Aaron said to all the Israelites, "In the evening you will know that it was the LORD who brought you out of Egypt, and in the morning you will see the glory of the LORD, because he has heard your grumbling against him. Who are we, that you should grumble against us?" Moses also said, "You will know that it was the LORD when he gives you meat to eat in the evening and all the bread you want in the morning, because he has heard your grumbling against him. Who are we? You are not grumbling against us, but against the LORD."

How quickly we forget

Suffering sears the human spirit so fully that we begin to believe lies about the past and, even more dangerous, the future becomes a dead wasteland in our clouded vision. We tend to doubt God's goodness when we follow him through difficult experiences. God cares for us beyond imagination. Although we know this, how do we feel it when our guts tighten with fear and a sense of abandonment?

The moment the Israelites didn't get the food they craved, they began to blame Moses and Aaron. How quickly they forgot the God who had brought them out of Egypt. Though the Israelites remembered Egypt fondly and blamed their deliverer, the Almighty still chose to provide them with what they needed.

Provision doesn't always arrive as tangibly as manna from heaven. Sometimes we forget that the world groans under the weight of a curse and that God's love doesn't instantly remove all discomfort from our lives. But hidden in God's nature we find answers. When the world threatens to crush our hope, we must cling to the knowledge of God's goodness. Then we can see our situation clearly as daughters of a heavenly Father who desires our good more than we possibly can imagine.

When Samuel reached him, Saul said, "The Lord bless you! I have carried out the Lord's instructions."

But Samuel said, "What then is this bleating of sheep in my ears? What is this lowing of cattle that I hear?"

Saul answered, "The soldiers brought them from the Amalekites; they spared the best of the sheep and cattle to sacrifice to the Lord your God, but we totally destroyed the rest."

Samuel said, "The Lord anointed you king over Israel. And he sent you on a mission, saying, 'Go and completely destroy those wicked people, the Amalekites; make war on them until you have wiped them out.' Why did you not obey the Lord? Why did you pounce on the plunder and do evil in the eyes of the Lord?"

"But I did obey the Lord," Saul said.

But Samuel replied: "Does the Lord delight in burnt offerings and sacrifices as much as in obeying the voice of the Lord? To obey is better than sacrifice, and to heed is better than the fat of rams. Because you have rejected the word of the Lord, he has rejected you as king."

But, Lord!

Samuel, God's messenger on earth, gave Saul clear instructions: Wipe out all of the Amalekites and take no plunder. No exceptions. But Saul's actions revealed his self-willed heart: "But, Lord, I didn't think you meant all of them!" God's plans didn't fit Saul's plans so he tweaked them to fit his convenience.

We're all a little like Saul. We all fall into the "but, Lord" trap. "I know your grace is sufficient, but, Lord, I think I'll take the easy way out." "But, Lord, why can't I tell five of my best friends about what happened?" "But, Lord, surely flirting isn't cheating." "But, Lord, this chat room helps me escape my boring life." "But, Lord, overeating isn't hurting anyone else, is it?"

We dig ourselves in deeper when, instead of squelching temptation, we turn toward it. The turn starts when, like Saul, we respond to God's promptings within us with "But, Lord…" The more frequently we make that turn, the more we fool ourselves that we are innocent.

Our daily lives present us with ample opportunity to choose God's leading or to reject it. Saul chose to disobey, and it cost him the kingdom. Jesus chose to obey, and he gained the keys to the kingdom of heaven.

1 Corinthians 7:8-16

Now to the unmarried and the widows I say: It is good for them to stay unmarried, as I am. But if they cannot control themselves, they should marry, for it is better to marry than to burn with passion.

To the married I give this command (not I, but the Lord): A wife must not separate from her husband. But if she does, she must remain unmarried or else be reconciled to her husband. And a husband must not divorce his wife.

To the rest I say this (I, not the Lord): If any brother has a wife who is not a believer and she is willing to live with him, he must not divorce her. And if a woman has a husband who is not a believer

and he is willing to live with her, she must not divorce him. For the unbelieving husband has been sanctified through his wife, and the unbelieving wife has been sanctified through her believing husband. Otherwise your children would be unclean, but as it is, they are holy.

But if the unbeliever leaves, let him do so. A believing man or woman is not bound in such circumstances; God has called us to live in peace. How do you know, wife, whether you will save your husband? Or, how do you know, husband, whether you will save your wife?

No distractions

What are you doing right now that is keeping you from enjoying what God has for you? Satan will turn this plot around in a number of ways. For example, he often tries to get us so bothered by the one thing we have been commanded by God not to do, that we spend far too much time thinking about it. Ultimately it distracts us from obeying God in other areas. We become so preoccupied with certain restrictions that God has placed on our lives that we forget, just as Eve did, that those restrictions are for our own good.

What joy there is in simply enjoying what God has for us right now. But in order to do that, we must not be consumed with what he has asked us not to do.

If you are married, Satan seeks to make you powerless in your marriage. If you have children, Satan wants you to long to be free to do whatever you want at the risk of abandoning your family. If you are working in the ministry, he wants you to yearn for more money. Whatever it is that God has not called you to do right now in your life, Satan will do his best to entice you with that very thing. So, beware!

Miriam and Aaron began to talk against Moses because of his Cushite wife.

At once the LORD said to Moses, Aaron and Miriam, "Come out to the Tent of Meeting, all three of you." So the three of them came out. Then the LORD came down in a pillar of cloud; he stood at the entrance to the Tent and summoned Aaron and Miriam. When both of them stepped forward, he said, "Listen to my words:

"When a prophet of the LORD is among you, I reveal myself to him in visions, I speak to him in dreams. But this is not true of my servant Moses; he is faithful in all my house. With him I speak face to face, clearly and not in riddles; he sees the form of the LORD."

Boiling over

The root of jealousy is often insecurity. It's not so much a question of what's so special about someone else as it is a question of what's so un-special about me?

When Miriam and Aaron saw the way God was using Moses, they were jealous. They wanted to be what he was. And who wouldn't? God actually talked to Moses face-to-face. He had a unique role in history that no one else had ever played. But Miriam and Aaron also had unique roles in history—roles that Moses couldn't fill—roles that they alone could fill. Miriam was a prophetess. Think of how rare in that day—a female prophet! And Aaron was the high priest, the priest above all other priests.

God has made a place for you in his kingdom that only you can fill. You may be a Moses, out front leading the way. Or you may be serving in more behind-the-scenes ways like Miriam and Aaron. Your job is not to compare your work to that of another and attach value based on what you can see. Your job is to turn down the heat of jealousy and quietly go about the work God has given you to do.

The LORD sent Nathan to David. When he came to him, he said, "There were two men in a certain town, one rich and the other poor. The rich man had a very large number of sheep and cattle, but the poor man had nothing except one little ewe lamb he had bought. He raised it, and it grew up with him and his children. It shared his food, drank from his cup and even slept in his arms. It was like a daughter to him.

"Now a traveler came to the rich man, but the rich man refrained from taking one of his own sheep or cattle to prepare a meal for the traveler who had come to him. Instead, he took the ewe lamb that belonged to the poor man and prepared it for the one who had come to him."

David burned with anger against the man and said to Nathan, "As surely as the LORD lives, the man who did this deserves to die! He must pay for that lamb four times over, because he did such a thing and had no pity."

Then Nathan said to David, "You are the man!

"This is what the LORD says: 'Out of your own household I am going to bring calamity upon you.' "

Then David said to Nathan, "I have sinned against the LORD." Nathan replied, "The LORD has taken away your sin. You are not going to die. But because by doing this you have made the enemies of the LORD show utter contempt, the son born to you will die."

Cleansed by the light

Where do you go when you feel flawed? Where do you find healing when you know you are sick?

A missionary on the border between Thailand and Cambodia ministers to people suffering from leprosy in the refugee camps. He and his colleagues began to spend time with those men and women, doing what they could to aid them physically and spiritually. Eventually a church was born right there in the middle of a leper camp.

During one of the services a man who had been among the first to make a commitment to following Christ said, "One of the most wonderful things that has happened to me since I met Jesus is that now I can look you in the face. I was too ashamed before because of my disfigurement, but if Jesus loves me so much, then I think that I can hold my head up high."

That is how it is supposed to be for all of us. Jesus has restored our dignity. We all struggle with our humanity and with our selfishness, but cleansing is not found in the shadows; it is found in the burning light.

Psalm 71:1-7

In you, O LORD, I have taken refuge; let me never be put to shame.

Rescue me and deliver me in your righteousness; turn your ear to me and save me.

Be my rock of refuge, to which I can always go; give the command to save me, for you are my rock and my fortress.

Deliver me, O my God, from the hand of the wicked, from the grasp of evil and cruel men.

For you have been my hope, O Sovereign LORD, my confidence since my youth.

From birth I have relied on you; you brought me forth from my mother's womb. I will ever praise you.

I have become like a portent to many, but you are my strong refuge.

Unshakable confidence

What do you rely on to give you confidence? Your skills, your degrees, your accomplishments? What about when you sense a call to do a task for which you feel unqualified?

If we rely only on ourselves we will not be qualified for that which God calls us. God often chose people who felt unqualified for the tasks he laid before them. Abraham, Sarah, Moses, David, Esther and Mary all felt unequal to the task. But if God can use a roaming Bedouin to birth a nation, a stuttering speaker to confront Egypt's pharaoh, a shepherd boy to lead a nation, an exiled Jewish girl to rescue her people and a timid teenager to bear the Son of God, then God can use us! The critical question isn't, "Can I do this?" The better question is, "Can God do this through me. The answer is a resounding "Yes!"

When the psalmist asked God to be a refuge and a rescuer in Psalm 71, he boldly proclaimed his dependence on the Sovereign Lord. When we feel weak-kneed and lack confidence, we are most open to relying on God. The Bible gives us affirmation after affirmation of God's strength in the face of our limited ability. So, if you find yourself in a new situation today, make sure that you place your unshakable confidence in the limitless God.

When they had assembled, Paul said to them: "My brothers, although I have done nothing against our people or against the customs of our ancestors, I was arrested in Jerusalem and handed over to the Romans. They examined me and wanted to release me, because I was not guilty of any crime deserving death. But when the Jews objected, I was compelled to appeal to Caesar—not that I had any charge to bring against my own people. For this reason I have asked to see you and talk with you. It is because of the hope of Israel that I am bound with this chain."

They replied, "We have not received any letters from Judea concerning you, and none of the brothers who have come from there has reported or said anything bad about you. But we want to hear what your views are, for we know that people everywhere are talking against this sect."

The power of pain

Suffering and pain can lead to powerful ministry. Amy Carmichael established a home to rescue children from prostitution in India. When she fell ill and was confined to bed she wrote inspirational poems that continue to encourage generations of readers.

Our Father knows what's best for us, so why should we complain?
We always want the sunshine, but he knows there must be rain.
We love the sound of laughter, and the merriment of cheer
But our hearts would lose their tenderness if we never shed a tear. ...
God never hurts us needlessly, and he never wastes our pain,
For every loss he sends to us is followed by rich gain. ...

When he was in chains Paul preached to the Roman Jews and many of them believed in Jesus. He also wrote many letters, including the joy-filled letter to the Philippians, from a jail cell.

We have all experienced suffering. No matter how universal the trauma, your situation and your response are personal to you. Others can learn from what you have gone through. Ask God for opportunities to share what you've learned about God's grace through your experience with suffering. Then stand back and be amazed at how God can use you to touch other people's lives.

Joel 2:25-27

"I will repay you for the years the locusts have eaten—the great locust and the young locust, the other locusts and the locust swarm — my great army that I sent among you.

You will have plenty to eat, until you are full, and you will praise the name of the LORD your God, who has worked wonders for you; never again will my people be shamed.

Then you will know that I am in Israel, that I am the LORD your God, and that there is no other; never again will my people be shamed."

But for a moment

After the wicked King Louis XIV of France revoked the Edict of Nantes and condemned tens of thousands of the noblest men and women of France to torture and death, many brave women were imprisoned in a terrible dungeon.

When at last the Huguenot women were released in 1768 someone found a word carved in the middle of the hard stone floor. That one word was Resist. It is thought that some woman carved it to help and strengthen herself and others so that after she was gone they might be encouraged in their resolve to endure till the end. Can the God who so gloriously nourished these women with heavenly strength not feed us also, in our lesser needs, as we wait day by day upon him?

When we think of suffering such as myriads have endured in all ages, in all lands, and of the suffering that many are enduring today, our own little troubles and difficulties seem too small to think about at all, and we can only find relief in praying for those who suffer. And yet, sometimes our trifles can try us a good deal, and those words, "And even this shall pass," may bring comfort. Remember, at its longest it is "but for a moment."

"Samaria did not commit half the sins you did. You have done more detestable things than they, and have made your sisters seem righteous by all these things you have done. Bear your disgrace, for you have furnished some justification for your sisters. Because your sins were more vile than theirs, they appear more righteous than you. So then, be ashamed and bear your disgrace, for you have made your sisters appear righteous.

"You are now scorned by the daughters of Edom and all her neighbors and the daughters of the Philistines—all those around you who despise you. You will bear the consequences of your lewdness and your detestable practices," declares the LORD.

"Then, when I make atonement for you for all you have done, you will remember and be ashamed and never again open your mouth because of your humiliation, declares the Sovereign LORD.' "

Turn around

*C*hoices determine the course of a life. They can establish the legacy of a family. And they can affect the destiny of a nation. Wise choices will bring blessings; foolish ones will bring destruction and pain. Some choices can cost us nearly everything.

This passage tells an allegory of how the people of Jerusalem betrayed God. The language paints a picture of a loving God who had compassion on people who had nothing of their own, who were alone and helpless. God's tender care is beautiful to see. But as the story continues we are shocked. The people betray God. They abandon their savior and pursue other gods. God's love is spurned by the people's willful and selfish choices.

Maybe you've made some poor choices too. Have you chosen to walk your own road, going against what you know to be right? God will deal with you. There is no getting around that. He loves you too much to leave you to follow your own ways or the ways of the world. The next choice you make could be the one that changes your life. Instead of going your own way, return to the Lover of your soul.

But Christ has indeed been raised from the dead, the first fruits of those who have fallen asleep. For since death came through a man, the resurrection of the dead comes also through a man. For as in Adam all die, so in Christ all will be made alive. But each in his own turn: Christ, the first fruits; then, when he comes, those who belong to him. Then the end will come, when he hands over the kingdom to God the Father after he has destroyed all dominion, authority and power. For he must reign until he has put all his enemies under his feet. The last enemy to be destroyed is death.

I declare to you, brothers, that flesh and blood cannot inherit the kingdom of God, nor does the perishable inherit the imperishable. Listen, I tell you a mystery: We will not all sleep, but we will all be changed—in a flash, in the twinkling of an eye, at the last trumpet. For the trumpet will sound, the dead will be raised imperishable, and we will be changed.

Why the resurrection matters

When C.S. Lewis lost his wife to cancer he wrote, "How often—will it be for always?—how often will the vast emptiness astonish me like a complete novelty and make me say, 'I never realized my loss till this moment?' The same leg is cut off time after time. The first plunge of the knife into the flesh is felt again and again."

It's normal—and healthy—to grieve when those we love are taken from us. But in 1 Corinthians 15 Paul explains why the resurrection of Jesus matters so much to those who believe that this earthly chapter is not the end of the eternal story. The pain of death will one day be only a memory.

When we leave our physical bodies behind we'll be ushered into God's presence where we'll feel his healing embrace. We'll be enveloped by his all-consuming love. And suddenly, in the light of God's face, and in the face of his passion for us, all our questions, our grief and our sorrows, will fade away. And one day, at the resurrection, our perishable bodies will be "clothed with the imperishable."

If you are grieving, hold on to the promise of the resurrection. It will make all the difference in this world—and in the next.

I Kings 10:1-9

When the queen of Sheba heard about the fame of Solomon and his relation to the name of the LORD, she came to test him with hard questions. Arriving at Jerusalem with a very great caravan—with camels carrying spices, large quantities of gold, and precious stones—she came to Solomon and talked with him about all that she had on her mind. Solomon answered all her questions; nothing was too hard for the king to explain to her. When the queen of Sheba saw all the wisdom of Solomon and the palace he had built, the food on his table, the seating of his officials, the attending servants in their robes, his cupbearers, and the burnt offerings he made at the temple of the LORD, she was overwhelmed.

She said to the king, "The report I heard in my own country about your achievements and your wisdom is true. But I did not believe these things until I came and saw with my own eyes. Indeed, not even half was told me; in wisdom and wealth you have far exceeded the report I heard. How happy your men must be! How happy your officials, who continually stand before you and hear your wisdom! Praise be to the LORD your God, who has delighted in you and placed you on the throne of Israel. Because of the LORD's eternal love for Israel, he has made you king, to maintain justice and righteousness."

The woman who had everything

In 1 Kings we meet the exotic queen of Sheba who had heard of King Solomon and the wisdom he possessed. So this woman, the ruler of a great empire in southern Arabia, ordered her servants to pack up her belongings and traveled by camel caravan to see the king. But she didn't come empty-handed. Like the Magi visiting Jesus she came bearing gifts—spices, gold and precious stones.

As a politician she could have come to Solomon seeking a new trade route or asking for a peace treaty. But her purpose in making the long, grueling journey was clear. The queen was on a spiritual quest, wanting to learn about Solomon's God. So she "talked with him about all that she had on her mind."

Do you have questions for God that you think he cannot or will not answer? Rest assured that God is not offended when you come to him with your candid questions. He knows that wisdom is more valuable than any treasure on earth. You don't need to be the queen of a nation or travel to a distant land to seek the answers to your heartfelt questions; you simply need to open the pages of God's Word and go to him in prayer.

Zechariah 7:8-14

*And the word of the L*ORD *came again to Zechariah: "This is what the L*ORD *Almighty says: 'Administer true justice; show mercy and compassion to one another. Do not oppress the widow or the fatherless, the alien or the poor. In your hearts do not think evil of each other.'*

*"But they refused to pay attention; stubbornly they turned their backs and stopped up their ears. They made their hearts as hard as flint and would not listen to the law or to the words that the L*ORD *Almighty had sent by his Spirit through the earlier prophets. So the L*ORD *Almighty was very angry.*

*" ' When I called, they did not listen; so when they called, I would not listen,' says the L*ORD *Almighty. 'I scattered them with a whirlwind among all the nations, where they were strangers. The land was left so desolate behind them that no one could come or go. This is how they made the pleasant land desolate.' "*

Failure to communicate

The Israelites had a massive breakdown in communication with God. They did not listen when he called them. So when they finally called upon him, he would not listen to them. They did not avail themselves of the relationship God wanted with them. They thought they would avoid the consequences of miscommunication. Instead, God was unreachable for a time. They ended up in a land of desolation.

Desolation—a sorry sort of word, a sorry sort of life. We each know what that looks like and it's not an inviting image. We don't really want to end up desolate and unheard, as the Israelites did, but how do we avoid it? How do we listen to God?

The Word of God is the framework from which we listen. When we know it and absorb it, it is dynamic and living. Scripture intersects with our thoughts, feelings and spirit. We create an open space for that to happen by dedicating time and attention to study and prayer. Out of love and respect for God, we concentrate on listening to him—as if he were the only other being in the universe. Listening means that we are receptive; like soft ground that soaks up the rain, so the Word can yield rich fruit in our lives.

First, I thank my God through Jesus Christ for all of you, because your faith is being reported all over the world. God, whom I serve with my whole heart in preaching the gospel of his Son, is my witness how constantly I remember you in my prayers at all times; and I pray that now at last by God's will the way may be opened for me to come to you.

I long to see you so that I may impart to you some spiritual gift to make you strong— that is, that you and I may be mutually encouraged by each other's faith. I do not want you to be unaware, brothers, that I planned many times to come to you (but have been prevented from doing so until now) in order that I might have a harvest among you, just as I have had among the other Gentiles.

I am obligated both to Greeks and non-Greeks, both to the wise and the foolish. That is why I am so eager to preach the gospel also to you who are at Rome.

I am not ashamed of the gospel, because it is the power of God for the salvation of everyone who believes: first for the Jew, then for the Gentile. For in the gospel a righteousness from God is revealed, a righteousness that is by faith from first to last, just as it is written: "The righteous will live by faith."

Not ashamed

We might be ashamed if our children get in trouble or if we fail to keep our temper. We may feel ashamed if we neglect prayer or realize we haven't done much for anyone but ourselves for a long while. Not to worry. God has freed us to walk in this world unashamed. In Christ there is forgiveness and a new start. In fact, there is only one real reason to be ashamed—if we're ashamed of the gospel message. Paul made sure that his readers knew he was not ashamed of the gospel. Indeed, he was eager to tell everyone about it.

Maybe you're embarrassed to let people know you are a Christian. Maybe you don't share your faith because you think your credentials aren't good enough. You're afraid that you don't have the right education or that you haven't memorized enough Scripture or that you haven't been a believer long enough. But think of the many people in the Bible who were saved and immediately went and told others about their encounter with Christ.

If you're not ashamed of Jesus, the best way to overcome the fear of speaking out is to "just do it." Talk to your neighbors, tell your friends and family, and share the story about how Jesus redeemed you.

You are always righteous, O LORD, when I bring a case before you. Yet I would speak with you about your justice: Why does the way of the wicked prosper? Why do all the faithless live at ease?

This is what the LORD says: "As for all my wicked neighbors who seize the inheritance I gave my people Israel, I will uproot them from their lands and I will uproot the house of Judah from among them. But after I uproot them, I will again have compassion and will bring each of them back to his own inheritance and his own country. And if they learn well the ways of my people and swear by my name, saying, 'As surely as the LORD lives'-even as they once taught my people to swear by Baal—then they will be established among my people. But if any nation does not listen, I will completely uproot and destroy it," declares the LORD.

Why do the wicked prosper?

We've all asked questions similar to Jeremiah's at least once. It's hard to understand why God appears to sanction those who openly disregard him. In Jeremiah's case it was people in his own hometown he was trying to help who had turned against him. They even plotted to kill him!

Sometimes we may feel that God has given a greater measure of his protection and provision to people who don't live upright lives. It's hard to reconcile God's nature when we see injustice all around us. We wonder why he doesn't intervene immediately to punish those who make sinful choices.

If you sometimes question God's action, you're in good company. Throughout history, God's people have wrestled with the same issues. We look at martyrs, missionaries and others serving God who experience horrible suffering and pain. Why do evildoers often seem to have the easiest lives, while people of faith struggle? Shouldn't it be the other way around? This side of heaven we may never be able to answer such questions.

Even so, we know our God is all-wise, all-knowing and just. He watches over us and will make everything right in its time. The key is for each of us to remain faithful to him until then.

Proverbs 6:20, 23-35

My son, keep your father's commands … for these commands are a lamp, this teaching is a light, and the corrections of discipline are the way to life, keeping you from the immoral woman, from the smooth tongue of the wayward wife.

Do not lust in your heart after her beauty or let her captivate you with her eyes, for the prostitute reduces you to a loaf of bread, and the adulteress preys upon your very life.

Can a man scoop fire into his lap without his clothes being burned? Can a man walk on hot coals without his feet being scorched? So is he who sleeps with another man's wife; no one who touches her will go unpunished.

Men do not despise a thief if he steals to satisfy his hunger when he is starving. Yet if he is caught, he must pay sevenfold, though it costs him all the wealth of his house. But a man who commits adultery lacks judgment; whoever does so destroys himself. Blows and disgrace are his lot, and his shame will never be wiped away; for jealousy arouses a husband's fury, and he will show no mercy when he takes revenge. He will not accept any compensation; he will refuse the bribe, however great it is

Playing with fire

In the movie *Unfaithful* a married woman meets a younger man by chance on a Manhattan street. She is drawn to him and over the course of time begins an affair with him. Her husband finds out, and when he confronts his wife's lover, the husband kills him. It's a deeply disturbing movie portraying how a seemingly normal and average couple can become drawn into a web of lies and deception through random circumstances.

Even without events escalating into murder, adultery is still devastating. Adultery is a sin that isn't easily forgiven and is seldom forgotten by the injured spouse.

The Scripture warns that this sin, when committed in secrecy, can rarely be kept quiet, and when it does become known, the adulterer will have to face the fury of the betrayed spouse. The adulterer will experience disgrace and the kind of shame that will never be wiped away, and will have to live with a guilty conscience for the rest of his or her life. And even if the betrayed spouse decides to stay, the adulterer will have to prove his or her love and faithfulness for the rest of their marriage. Thus, adultery can reap a lifetime of consequences. The years of regret are not worth the momentary pleasure.

Psalm 95:1-11

Come, let us sing for joy to the LORD; let us shout aloud to the Rock of our salvation.
Let us come before him with thanksgiving and extol him with music and song.

For the LORD is the great God, the great King above all gods.
In his hand are the depths of the earth, and the mountain peaks belong to him.

The sea is his, for he made it, and his hands formed the dry land.
Come, let us bow down in worship, let us kneel before the LORD our Maker; for he is our God and we are the people of his pasture, the flock under his care.

Today, if you hear his voice, do not harden your hearts as you did at Meribah, as you did that day at Massah in the desert, where your fathers tested and tried me, though they had seen what I did.
For forty years I was angry with that generation; I said, "They are a people whose hearts go astray, and they have not known my ways."
So I declared on oath in my anger, "They shall never enter my rest."

Cue cards for praise

*P*salm 95 tells us to find companions as we praise. Marriage gives us one very important companion—someone to share all the exciting details, someone to cheer and sing and laugh with before the Lord.

Psalms is our songbook; the psalms our cue cards for praising God. Psalm 95 puts words in our mouths to express the joy in our hearts. And if our songs have gotten all mumbly and dull, this psalm helps us rejuvenate our singing together. We sing this kind of praise best when we gather with God's people in church. Don't miss such celebrations!

At home, try worshipping as a couple by recounting God's provision such as your first apartment or some unexpected money when things were tight. Praising God for his "shepherd care" is important for our future as a couple and as a family, for it is how we learn to trust God to guide us through the next dark valley or be our protection in a troubled tomorrow.

Psalm 95 ends by reminding us of what happens when we fail to let worship shape our will and our ways. What a great reminder to keep our marriages full of praise. When we worship God in our times of triumph, it prepares us to trust God in our times of struggle.

Hebrews 4:12-16

For the word of God is living and active. Sharper than any double-edged sword, it penetrates even to dividing soul and spirit, joints and marrow; it judges the thoughts and attitudes of the heart. Nothing in all creation is hidden from God's sight. Everything is uncovered and laid bare before the eyes of him to whom we must give account.

Therefore, since we have a great high priest who has gone through the heavens, Jesus the Son of God, let us hold firmly to the faith we profess. For we do not have a high priest who is unable to sympathize with our weaknesses, but we have one who has been tempted in every way, just as we are—yet was without sin. Let us then approach the throne of grace with confidence, so that we may receive mercy and find grace to help us in our time of need.

The throne of grace

Do you find it difficult to approach God when you encounter a tempting situation? How quickly do you come to him when your attitude needs adjustment or when you are about to engage in a habit you know is unhealthy?

Often our greatest comforters are those who have struggled with what we're facing. Why? Because they've been there. They've felt the pain, cried the buckets of tears, felt the anxiety and stayed up nights. They can sympathize in ways even our best friends cannot. But even their help is sometimes not enough. We need help from the throne of grace, the source of all comfort.

Jesus opened the way to forgiveness of sin and access to the Father. And beyond sympathy, Jesus offers empathy because he has suffered in ways no mere human has. Yes, Jesus encountered fear, exhaustion, weakness, abandonment and grief. He was misunderstood, mistreated, insulted, questioned, doubted and betrayed. Moreover, he suffered all the horror and terrors of punishment for our sin.

Jesus knows. He feels what you feel; he sees deep into your soul. You can approach his throne with confidence. He's waiting for you.

Genesis 50:15-21

When Joseph's brothers saw that their father was dead, they said, "What if Joseph holds a grudge against us and pays us back for all the wrongs we did to him?" So they sent word to Joseph, saying, "Your father left these instructions before he died: 'This is what you are to say to Joseph: I ask you to forgive your brothers the sins and the wrongs they committed in treating you so badly.' Now please forgive the sins of the servants of the God of your father." When their message came to him, Joseph wept.

His brothers then came and threw themselves down before him. "We are your slaves," they said.

But Joseph said to them, "Don't be afraid. Am I in the place of God? You intended to harm me, but God intended it for good to accomplish what is now being done, the saving of many lives. So then, don't be afraid. I will provide for you and your children." And he reassured them and spoke kindly to them.

A good gift from a good God

Sometimes our worry is the thread by which we hang onto the belief that we can do something to change our situation and end our fear. As ridiculous as it is, we believe that our anxiety gives us some measure of control. Or we believe that it keeps God mindful of our problem. If we don't worry, are we giving up hope of God involving himself in our world?

God's joy and peace are available to us as we trust him; they are not the result of absolute guarantees about the outcome of our worries. We have a choice: Will we trust him and receive his joy and peace, or will we insist on seeking our joy and peace from resolved fears and changed circumstances?

The choice really is ours. We can hang onto our fears, insisting that until they are resolved there is no way for us to enter into rest, or we can see those same fears as the door by which we can enter a rest far richer and sweeter than the rest that might arise from a tenuous arrangement of perfect circumstances. It is a rest that believes that a life without all the pieces in place is still a life to celebrate, a good gift from a good God.

If a member of the community sins unintentionally and does what is forbidden in any of the Lord's commands, he is guilty. When he is made aware of the sin he committed, he must bring as his offering for the sin he committed a female goat without defect. He is to lay his hand on the head of the sin offering and slaughter it at the place of the burnt offering. Then the priest is to take some of the blood with his finger and put it on the horns of the altar of burnt offering and pour out the rest of the blood at the base of the altar. He shall remove all the fat, just as the fat is removed from the fellowship offering, and the priest shall burn it on the altar as an aroma pleasing to the Lord. In this way the priest will make atonement for him, and he will be forgiven.

Don't-mean-it sins

Sometimes we sin without meaning it. We aim for righteousness, honor and wisdom, but we miss by a mile. Leviticus 4 introduces a Hebrew word for sin that means "to miss the mark." George R. Knight, professor of church history at Andrews Theological Seminary in Berrien Springs, Michigan, explains: "You have missed not because you are wicked, but because you are careless, inattentive, lazy, or more probably because you do not possess the proper aim in life."

Add to that Hebrew word for sin the word "unintentional" and it suggests someone wandering away like a sheep or someone who isn't thinking. We sometimes feel we ought to be given a break if we really didn't mean to sin. But the Bible doesn't cut us any slack. Whether we mean it or not, sin damages our relationship with God and with others.

Forgiveness is available, but it doesn't come cheap. Today, we who confess Jesus Christ as Savior are grateful that we don't have to go through the laborious and gruesome atonement rituals of the Old Testament. Still, as we read through the requirements in Leviticus, we realize how the sacrificial system illustrates the seriousness of sin. Sin is terrible—even when it's unintentional. Praise God that Christ's death provides forgiveness.

Hezekiah was twenty-five years old when he became king, and he reigned in Jerusalem twenty-nine years. His mother's name was Abijah daughter of Zechariah. He did what was right in the eyes of the LORD, just as his father David had done.

In the first month of the first year of his reign, he opened the doors of the temple of the LORD and repaired them. He brought in the priests and the Levites, assembled them in the square on the east side and said: "Listen to me, Levites! Consecrate yourselves now and consecrate the temple of the LORD, the God of your fathers. Remove all defilement from the sanctuary. Our fathers were unfaithful; they did evil in the eyes of the LORD our God and forsook him. They turned their faces away from the LORD's dwelling place and turned their backs on him. They also shut the doors of the portico and put out the lamps. They did not burn incense or present any burnt offerings at the sanctuary to the God of Israel. Therefore, the anger of the LORD has fallen on Judah and Jerusalem; he has made them an object of dread and horror and scorn, as you can see with your own eyes. This is why our fathers have fallen by the sword and why our sons and daughters and our wives are in captivity. Now I intend to make a covenant with the LORD, the God of Israel, so that his fierce anger will turn away from us. My sons, do not be negligent now, for the LORD has chosen you to stand before him and serve him, to minister before him and to burn incense."

First things first

What would you do if you were elected president of the United States? What would be the first thing on your official "to do" list?

Hezekiah was only 25 years old when he became king of Judah. His first priority was to repair the temple and reestablish worship, helping the people reconnect with God.

Most likely you will not be chosen to rule a country, but you are the queen of your castle—your home. So what is the first thing on your "to do" list each day? What is your number one priority? Eliminate your kids' hunger? Disarm family disputes? Tackle the budget? Or when you get up, do you put your house in order by first putting your heart in order? The best way to run a home, a business or a country is from your knees in prayer.

Take a cue from Hezekiah who gave his relationship with God top priority. Like Hezekiah, we have only a short time to make a difference to those in our small kingdoms. We cannot afford not to avail ourselves of God's wisdom and strength. Open the doors of your heart's temple and keep them open as you go about your day.

Philippians 4:4-13

Rejoice in the Lord always. I will say it again: Rejoice! Let your gentleness be evident to all. The Lord is near. Do not be anxious about anything, but in everything, by prayer and petition, with thanksgiving, present your requests to God. And the peace of God, which transcends all understanding, will guard your hearts and your minds in Christ Jesus.

Finally, brothers, whatever is true, whatever is noble, whatever is right, whatever is pure, whatever is lovely, whatever is admirable—if anything is excellent or praiseworthy—think about such things. Whatever you have learned or received or heard from me, or seen in me—put it into practice. And the God of peace will be with you.

I rejoice greatly in the Lord that at last you have renewed your concern for me. Indeed, you have been concerned, but you had no opportunity to show it. I am not saying this because I am in need, for I have learned to be content whatever the circumstances. I know what it is to be in need, and I know what it is to have plenty. I have learned the secret of being content in any and every situation, whether well fed or hungry, whether living in plenty or in want. I can do everything through him who gives me strength.

A gentle spirit

I f you walked down the street and asked five people what they thought the word gentleness meant, how many would say that a gentle person is docile, easily intimidated or passive? Or that gentleness would be a good quality for a pet or a horse? In our culture, assertiveness and forthrightness are more highly-valued personality traits for human beings than gentleness.

But the Scriptures value gentleness. Here Paul explains what it means to be virtuous, especially in view of the disputes that had arisen among the Philippians.

Paul reminded the Philippians that the key to peace was grateful prayer. He admonished them to give their every anxiety over to God as they gave thanks. More than that, Paul encouraged his readers—and us—to focus on things that are beautiful, pure and positive. Meditating on such things develops our ability to notice and appreciate small beauties and increases a sense of thanksgiving to God. A spirit of contentment and gratitude brings peace.

A woman who speaks words of encouragement and has an attitude of contentment is inviting; she draws people to her, even if she faces times of crisis and pain. When your gentleness is evident to all, others will know that the Lord is near and they, too, will rejoice.

Exodus 7:1-5, 20-24

Then the LORD said to Moses, "See, I have made you like God to Pharaoh, and your brother Aaron will be your prophet. You are to say everything I command you, and your brother Aaron is to tell Pharaoh to let the Israelites go out of his country. But I will harden Pharaoh's heart, and though I multiply my miraculous signs and wonders in Egypt, he will not listen to you. Then I will lay my hand on Egypt and with mighty acts of judgment I will bring out my divisions, my people the Israelites. And the Egyptians will know that I am the LORD when I stretch out my hand against Egypt and bring the Israelites out of it." ...

Moses and Aaron did just as the LORD had commanded. He raised his staff in the presence of Pharaoh and his officials and struck the water of the Nile, and all the water was changed into blood. The fish in the Nile died, and the river smelled so bad that the Egyptians could not drink its water. Blood was everywhere in Egypt.

But the Egyptian magicians did the same things by their secret arts, and Pharaoh's heart became hard; he would not listen to Moses and Aaron, just as the LORD had said. Instead, he turned and went into his palace, and did not take even this to heart. And all the Egyptians dug along the Nile to get drinking water, because they could not drink the water of the river.

Let his people go

Reading about the plagues and Pharaoh's hard-hearted responses can leave us frustrated. Why did Moses and Aaron have to go through all that hoopla? Why did the Egyptians have to suffer plague after plague? The answer is clear: "The Egyptians will know that I am the Lord when I stretch out my hand against Egypt and bring the Israelites out of it." God was just as concerned with the Egyptians as he was with the Israelites.

Yes, God wanted to free the Israelites from years of cruel bondage. But he wanted everyone—Egyptians and Israelites alike—to experience his power as the one true God.

Today, God still wants everyone to know that he is the only true God. And he shows his power through the events and circumstances of our lives. When we see the miracles of God, do we share those happenings with others? God still wants all people to know him. Unlike the black-and-white world portrayed in TV shows and movies, God goes beyond our expectations and spends time showing the Egyptians and Israelites about himself. So, the next time you see God reveal himself to you, don't hesitate to share your experiences with others—even those you might think don't have time for God.

Leviticus 10:1-3

Aaron's sons Nadab and Abihu took their censers, put fire in them and added incense; and they offered unauthorized fire before the LORD, contrary to his command. So fire came out from the presence of the LORD and consumed them, and they died before the LORD. Moses then said to Aaron, "This is what the LORD spoke of when he said: 'Among those who approach me I will show myself holy; in the sight of all the people I will be honored.' "

Holy Fire

We can't always see the reasons for God's requirements. Nadab and Abihu might have assumed that a good intention would find favor equal to obedience; perhaps God would even reward them for their ingenuity. As high priest, Aaron made the burnt offering decreed by God. But then Nadab and Abihu offered their own "unauthorized fire." The sacrifice had already been offered. God's glory had appeared. Nadab and Abihu presumptuously tried to add to God's decree for sacrifice. The result? Instant death. Verse 3 takes us to the heart of the matter: The closer we come to God, the more we must honor his holiness by obeying his commands.

As women, we face numerous opportunities to second-guess God. We justify detours from God's will by believing we're following the spirit of the law in our own creative way. But our ways are not God's ways. That's why obedience to God and what his Word tells us is crucial. Obedience shows God that we consider him holy and worthy of honor.

When God says something to you in his Word, take it personally. For example, reading the passage on honoring your husband or taming your tongue doesn't fulfill your obligation; your actions reflect your heart toward God. Obedience honors God. Disobedience dishonors him.

Proverbs 31:10-21, 25

*A wife of noble character
who can find? She is worth
far more than rubies.*

*Her husband has full confidence
in her and lacks nothing of value.*

*She brings him good, not
harm, all the days of her life.*

*She selects wool and flax and
works with eager hands.*

*She is like the merchant ships,
bringing her food from afar.*

*She gets up while it is still dark;
she provides food for her family
and portions for her servant girls.*

*She considers a field and
buys it; out of her earn-
ings she plants a vineyard.*

*She sets about her work vigorously;
her arms are strong for her tasks.*

*She sees that her trading
is profitable, and her lamp
does not go out at night.*

*In her hand she holds the
distaff and grasps the
spindle with her fingers.*

*She opens her arms to
the poor and extends her
hands to the needy.*

*When it snows, she has no
fear for her household; for all
of them are clothed in scarlet.*

*She is clothed with strength
and dignity; she can laugh
at the days to come.*

You gotta laugh

Unique challenges await the woman approaching middle age. Maybe you don't have to imagine it, maybe you're already there. God might have knit our bodies together out of a more permanent press kind of fabric. But he didn't, and through our aging and all the challenges we live through, he teaches us what's more important. The Proverbs 31 "virtuous woman" got in on that teaching. She could laugh at the days to come. Her future held flabby abs and thighs, too, but she could still laugh. Why?

The passage describes a woman who seems just about perfect. She is a formidable pattern, an intimidating example. But look past the outward layer. Look deeper and you'll see a woman of wisdom who fully understood what was really important. She understood what it meant to work hard and to serve God with her whole heart. She understood that everything of consequence was wrapped up in him. Serving others came as a natural extension of serving him.

There's only one metamorphosis that matters—and it will keep every woman eternally beautiful. It's a metamorphosis of the heart. Having a heart of unselfish service that has been transformed by Christ is what's important. And that is what gives us the ability to laugh at the future.

Therefore say: "This is what the Sovereign Lord says: Although I sent them far away among the nations and scattered them among the countries, yet for a little while I have been a sanctuary for them in the countries where they have gone."

This is what the Sovereign Lord says: "I will gather you from the nations and bring you back from the countries where you have been scattered, and I will give you back the land of Israel again.

"They will return to it and remove all its vile images and detestable idols. I will give them an undivided heart and put a new spirit in them; I will remove from them their heart of stone and give them a heart of flesh. Then they will follow my decrees and be careful to keep my laws. They will be my people, and I will be their God. But as for those whose hearts are devoted to their vile images and detestable idols, I will bring down on their own heads what they have done," declares the Sovereign Lord.

Shelter in a strange land

The past two centuries have produced an unprecedented shrinking of time and distance. Journeys that once required days or weeks have now been reduced to hours. Yet the availability of modern means of travel has also introduced a new level of fragmentation. As a result, you sometimes feel isolated from your friends and family. Though you long for closeness with others, you often find only loneliness.

The Israelites had slavery to add to their dislocation anxiety. God scattered them among foreign nations, fulfilling his promise to send them into captivity if they forgot to keep him first and foremost in their lives. In strange lands, far from temple life and the comfort of communal worship, God promised to be their sanctuary in the midst of their isolation.

Following Christ can be a lonely journey in a hostile world. Many of us can relate to feelings of abiding isolation not too different from the Israelites' alien existence as they groaned before God. God wants us to learn an important lesson from these seasons of loneliness: Our true citizenship is in heaven. When you feel like an outsider, remember that you are this citizen of heaven, and God promises to be your sanctuary in these foreign lands.

Matthew 16:13-16

When Jesus came to the region of Caesarea Philippi, he asked his disciples, "Who do people say the Son of Man is?"

They replied, "Some say John the Baptist; others say Elijah; and still others, Jeremiah or one of the prophets."

"But what about you?" he asked. "Who do you say I am?"

Simon Peter answered, "You are the Christ, the Son of the living God."

Jesus: our everything

"**J**esus is everything." These words of Mother Teresa were demonstrated by her selfless, Christ-like actions. She was a friend to the poor, unabashedly loving society's rejects and giving hope to the hopeless in her adopted country of India.

In Matthew 16, Jesus asked his disciples who they thought he was. Peter aced the pop quiz, calling him the son of the living God. We all know that Peter wasn't perfect. He was the one who denied Christ at Jesus' trial. Yet at this key moment he comprehended that Jesus was the Messiah God had promised. After Pentecost, Peter's boldness allowed him to proclaim Christ's identity whenever and wherever he could, regardless of the persecution and suffering it invited. Eventually, he was crucified for spreading the news that Jesus was God's Son.

The One who lived among us was God's hands and feet. He gave us the very words of his Father. He taught us how to love. He taught us how to give. And he taught us to die as a grain of wheat, so that the seeds of life are multiplied.

Mother Teresa and Peter understood that with Jesus there was no such thing as loving moderately. They showed others that Jesus was Lord of their lives by loving as he loved and serving as he served.

During harvest time, three of the thirty chief men came down to David at the cave of Adullam, while a band of Philistines was encamped in the Valley of Rephaim. At that time David was in the stronghold, and the Philistine garrison was at Bethlehem. David longed for water and said, "Oh, that someone would get me a drink of water from the well near the gate of Bethlehem!" So the three mighty men broke through the Philistine lines, drew water from the well near the gate of Bethlehem and carried it back to David. But he refused to drink it; instead, he poured it out before the LORD. "Far be it from me, O LORD, to do this!" he said. "Is it not the blood of men who went at the risk of their lives?" And David would not drink it.

Such were the exploits of the three mighty men.

153

Sacrificing for each other

Having a healthy marriage requires sacrifices. Maybe you are living on a tight budget. Maybe you've moved far away from family and friends for your spouse's job. Or maybe you've let go of a personal dream so that the two of you can build new dreams together. We make these sacrifices because we know that the loss is tempered by an even greater gain.

It's ironic, then, that we tend to be resistant to sacrificing for God. Where we might not hesitate to make a change for the sake of our spouses, how many of us are willing to make the kind of deep, life-altering changes that will help us become the people God created us to be?

The story of David's mighty warriors provides a good example of people willing to risk everything for a person they cared about. After reading this story, one wonders if the mighty men would have risked their lives if God had been doing the asking. Would we?

When we become more devoted to our marriage than to God we have lost sight of God's real desire for us—that we be people of love, compassion and mercy, people who put everything aside and follow the Lord.

1 Samuel 1:1-8

There was a certain man from Ramathaim, a Zuphite from the hill country of Ephraim, whose name was Elkanah son of Jeroham, the son of Elihu, the son of Tohu, the son of Zuph, an Ephraimite. He had two wives; one was called Hannah and the other Peninnah. Peninnah had children, but Hannah had none.

Year after year this man went up from his town to worship and sacrifice to the Lord Almighty at Shiloh, where Hophni and Phinehas, the two sons of Eli, were priests of the Lord. Whenever the day came for Elkanah to sacrifice, he would give portions of the meat to his wife Peninnah and to all her sons and daughters. But to Hannah he gave a double portion because he loved her, and the Lord had closed her womb. And because the Lord had closed her womb, her rival kept provoking her in order to irritate her. This went on year after year. Whenever Hannah went up to the house of the Lord, her rival provoked her till she wept and would not eat. Elkanah her husband would say to her, "Hannah, why are you weeping? Why don't you eat? Why are you downhearted? Don't I mean more to you than ten sons?"

When your love isn't enough

Elkanah meant well. He realized that his wife was upset and hurting from her inability to get pregnant. Added to that, Hannah had to deal with the daily taunts of Elkanah's other wife who had plenty of children. Elkanah asked, "Am I not enough? Isn't my wonderful, huge, spilling-over-into-everything love enough?" Hannah's answer was clear: "No, Elkanah, it's not enough."

We are so often tempted, like Elkanah, to think that the love we offer in marriage is enough to meet our spouse's every need. We mean well. When our spouse is feeling lonely or has had a bad day at work, we want to fix things. We want our love to take away whatever the hurt is. But people have needs and desires that a spouse can't meet, such as a desire related to a job, or a desire for friendship.

When we allow married love to be what it is supposed to be—important but not all-important, meaningful but not all-meaningful, a priority but not the only priority—and when we stop looking to our spouse to be more than he or she can be, then we are better able to appreciate the ways marriage does fulfill us.

Psalm 103:8-18

*The LORD is compassionate
and gracious, slow to anger,
abounding in love.*

*He will not always accuse, nor
will he harbor his anger forever; he does not treat us as
our sins deserve or repay us
according to our iniquities.*

*For as high as the heavens are
above the earth, so great is his
love for those who fear him;
as far as the east is from the
west, so far has he removed
our transgressions from us.*

*As a father has compassion on his
children, so the LORD has compassion on those who fear him; for
he knows how we are formed, he
remembers that we are dust.*

*As for man, his days are like
grass, he flourishes like a flower
of the field; the wind blows
over it and it is gone, and its
place remembers it no more.*

*But from everlasting to everlasting
the LORD's love is with those who
fear him, and his righteousness
with their children's children—with
those who keep his covenant and
remember to obey his precepts.*

Grow up, not old

"I used to be cute, but now I feel invisible," said the fifty-something woman as she laughed nervously, but while her eyes glistened with tears. A thirty-something woman expressed the same feelings, saying, "When I was in my twenties I turned a few heads, but now, hey, I'm a mom of four. What can I expect?" Both women are attractive, some might say they are beautiful. But they each struggle with their self-image because our culture is not kind to aging women. Physical beauty and glamorized sexuality are prized above character and inner loveliness.

God's view—the biblical view—of growing older makes the world's view of beauty seem silly and nonsensical. But it takes mental discipline to focus on God's standards of worth and beauty when so many media outlets suggest that anyone over thirty is past their prime.

God doesn't pretend that growing older is easy. He acknowledges that our days are as fleeting as the grass growing in the field. We all realize that our outward beauty will fade away like a flower that blooms for a season and then disappears. Thankfully, our heavenly Father values the inner beauty that will never perish, an eternal beauty that comes from a heart radiating with God's love.

2 Chronicles 22:10-12

When Athaliah the mother of Ahaziah saw that her son was dead, she proceeded to destroy the whole royal family of the house of Judah. But Jehosheba, the daughter of King Jehoram, took Joash son of Ahaziah and stole him away from among the royal princes who were about to be murdered and put him and his nurse in a bedroom. Because Jehosheba, the daughter of King Jehoram and wife of the priest Jehoiada, was Ahaziah's sister, she hid the child from Athaliah so she could not kill him. He remained hidden with them at the temple of God for six years while Athaliah ruled the land.

Make a difference

C an one woman really make a difference in a community? What about in an entire nation? You might think the answer is no, but think again. When you read the story of Jehosheba you'll see that the answer is a wholehearted yes.

When Jehosheba realized that Athaliah was determined to destroy the royal line of Judah, she bravely hid her nephew Joash in the temple until he was old enough to succeed to the throne. When Joash was seven years old, he ascended to the throne and later repaired the temple and tore down the altars to Baal. More important, he preserved the Messianic line.

You may not see yourself as a woman of influence. You may feel shy about sharing your faith with your kids, friends, family or coworkers. But there are many ways you can make a difference. You can refuse to give in to peer pressure or refuse to give up on a prodigal. You can speak out in the voting booth or on the editorial page. When you stand up for God's standards, you might be surprised—like a small pebble thrown into a large body of water, your words, actions and prayers can ripple outward to others.

Psalm 13:1-6

How long, O LORD? Will you forget me forever?
How long will you hide your face from me?
How long must I wrestle with my thoughts and every day have sorrow
*   in my heart?*
How long will my enemy triumph over me?
Look on me and answer, O LORD my God.
Give light to my eyes, or I will sleep in death; my enemy will say, "I have
overcome him," and my foes will rejoice when I fall.
But I trust in your unfailing love; my heart rejoices in your salvation.
I will sing to the LORD, for he has been good to me.

Never alone

*I*n this psalm, the writer found himself feeling so alone, so seemingly abandoned by God, that he was plunged into a deep depression and despair that took him to the edge of death. He was wrestling with his thoughts. His sorrow was overwhelming. Perhaps you can relate to such feelings. Perhaps you know what it's like when your thoughts are whirling around in aching confusion.

Then comes the "but." The psalmist, even as he was suffering terribly, stopped himself with that one little word. He chose to trust in God's goodness even when his heart was failing and grieving. Because he knew God, he chose to trust in God's unfailing love and rejoice even in the midst of sorrow.

The psalmist made a choice. He made a conscious decision to trust in God's love even when the dark clouds of terror and depression hid God's face. The psalmist knew this as a fact. And you can know it too. You are never alone, God is always nearby, even when you can't see his face or feel his presence. When you feel alone, call out to him. No matter how you feel, the fact remains that he is here. He is everywhere. And he hears your cries.

Then Jesus was led by the Spirit into the desert to be tempted by the devil. After fasting forty days and forty nights, he was hungry. The tempter came to him and said, "If you are the Son of God, tell these stones to become bread."

Jesus answered, "It is written: 'Man does not live on bread alone, but on every word that comes from the mouth of God.' "

Then the devil took him to the holy city and had him stand on the highest point of the temple. "If you are the Son of God," he said, "throw yourself down. For it is written: 'He will command his angels concerning you, and they will lift you up in their hands, so that you will not strike your foot against a stone.' "

Jesus answered him, "It is also written: 'Do not put the Lord your God to the test.' "

Again, the devil took him to a very high mountain and showed him all the kingdoms of the world and their splendor. "All this I will give you," he said, "if you will bow down and worship me."

Jesus said to him, "Away from me, Satan! For it is written: 'Worship the Lord your God, and serve him only.' "

Confronting temptation

Jesus was tempted to sin but, unlike us, he never succumbed. The most striking episode of Jesus resisting temptation is recorded in Matthew 4. After fasting for forty days and nights, and when he was physically at his weakest, Jesus was approached by Satan. The devil wasted no time attacking the human motives that most often lead people to sin.

Every person alive is tempted in these same areas: physical needs, personal identity and personal possessions. For the most part, our culture tells us to satisfy our needs any way we can. But as God's people, we are taught to align our choices with God's ideas of how to control our physical drives, to see ourselves in relation to him, and to rightly handle our possessions.

The ways Jesus responded to temptation offer us good weapons for our own struggles to resist the lures of Satan. For example, Jesus consistently used Scripture to respond to Satan. When tempted to satisfy a physical drive, Jesus pointed out the importance of seeking satisfaction in God's Word rather than earthly food. And he responded to Satan's attempts to make him glorify himself or to own worldly possessions by saying, in essence, "Don't give priority to yourself or to things. You are to worship God and serve him only."

Bathsheba went to see the aged king in his room, where Abishag the Shunammite was attending him. Bathsheba bowed low and knelt before the king. What is it you want?" the king asked.

She said to him, "My Lord, you yourself swore to me your servant by the LORD your God: 'Solomon your son shall be king after me, and he will sit on my throne.' But now Adonijah has become king, and you, my lord the king, do not know about it."

While she was still speaking with the king, Nathan the prophet arrived. And they told the king, "Nathan the prophet is here." So he went before the king and bowed with his face to the ground.

Nathan said, "Have you, my lord the king, declared that Adonijah shall be king after you, and that he will sit on your throne? Is this something my LORD the king has done without letting his servants know who should sit on the throne of my lord the king after him?"

Then King David said, "Call in Bathsheba." So she came into the king's presence and stood before him.

The king then took an oath: "As surely as the LORD lives, who has delivered me out of every trouble, I will surely carry out today what I swore to you by the LORD, the God of Israel: Solomon your son shall be king after me, and he will sit on my throne in my place."

'Fessing up

When David was close to death, his son Adonijah made his move to take over the kingdom. Although this was a pivotal moment in David and Adonijah's relationship, and in the story of Israel, the two failed to communicate about what was really important.

Isn't that usually the way we handle life? We can talk with the people close to us about politics, the weather, vacation plans or the TV shows we like best. But in the midst of major transitions we sometimes fail to talk things through with the people who matter the most to us.

It's easy to avoid conversations about important things. But when we neglect to share our pivotal points in life, especially with our spouse, we are really saying, "I am keeping this for myself. I am not willing to give you my whole self—not the parts that really matter." It's like refusing to bring our pivotal points to God. We may say we love him, and we may be doing our best to obey him. But when we withhold some of the things we are struggling with, what we are really saying is, "You can have everything else, but not this. Here, where it really matters, I'll find my own way and do as I please."

Nehemiah 4:7-10, 13-18

But when Sanballat, Tobiah, the Arabs, the Ammonites and the men of Ashdod heard that the repairs to Jerusalem's walls had gone ahead and that the gaps were being closed, they were very angry. They all plotted together to come and fight against Jerusalem and stir up trouble against it. But we prayed to our God and posted a guard day and night to meet this threat.

Meanwhile, the people in Judah said, "The strength of the laborers is giving out, and there is so much rubble that we cannot rebuild the wall."

Therefore I stationed some of the people behind the lowest points of the wall at the exposed places, posting them by families, with their swords, spears and bows. After I looked things over, I stood up and said to the nobles, the officials and the rest of the people, "Don't be afraid of them.

Remember the LORD, who is great and awesome, and fight for your brothers, your sons and your daughters, your wives and your homes."

When our enemies heard that we were aware of their plot and that God had frustrated it, we all returned to the wall, each to his own work.

From that day on, half of my men did the work, while the other half were equipped with spears, shields, bows and armor. The officers posted themselves behind all the people of Judah who were building the wall. Those who carried materials did their work with one hand and held a weapon in the other, and each of the builders wore his sword at his side as he worked. But the man who sounded the trumpet stayed with me.

Persistence pays

When the Jews listened to the taunts and insults of their enemies they felt their strength dissipating and even felt like giving up. It took the watchful eyes of Nehemiah to see the deeper spiritual realities—that God was greater than the enemy and that he would strengthen his people so that they could finish building the wall.

Nehemiah knew that enemies were plotting, so he summoned up strength by seeking the Lord. The simple phrase "but we prayed" serves as a clarion call to prayer when the work seems too hard and we feel like calling it quits. Think about it. If Nehemiah had given up, the walls of Jerusalem would not have been rebuilt.

What if Jesus had given up? We would not have a Savior to forgive our sins. Thankfully Jesus finished what he started. Through prayer you can carry on too, knowing that "he who began a good work in you will carry it on to completion until the day of Christ Jesus" (Philippians 1:6).

Genesis 16:1-4

Now Sarai, Abram's wife, had borne him no children. But she had an Egyptian maidservant named Hagar; so she said to Abram, "The LORD has kept me from having children. Go, sleep with my maidservant; perhaps I can build a family through her."

Abram agreed to what Sarai said. So after Abram had been living in Canaan ten years, Sarai his wife took her Egyptian maidservant Hagar and gave her to her husband to be his wife. He slept with Hagar, and she conceived.

Promises worth waiting for

What are you waiting for? Who or what do you believe will satisfy and complete you? You may be waiting for Mr. Right, your dream job, a precious baby or any number of things to fulfill your hopes and dreams. Waiting is hard when you just know your life will be so much better if your hopes become reality.

Sarai was fed up with waiting for the baby God had promised. She grew older every day and her body showed no sign of pregnancy. Perhaps she questioned that God's promise of children for Abraham included her. But God had a plan. A plan to bless Abraham and Sarai with their very own baby. That plan was worth waiting for.

God has plans for your life, too. Plans that will make you thrive and not be knocked down by life's setbacks (see Jeremiah 29:11-13). God's plans are well worth waiting for. You may be tempted to take matters in your own hands, thinking God is just a little bit late. But don't risk God's perfect intentions for you by relying on your own schemes. Waiting for God's perfect timing can save you years of heartbreak. Remember, God is faithful and always keeps his promises—even if you have to wait.

Some time later, Samson fell in love with a woman in the Valley of Sorek whose name was Delilah. The rulers of the Philistines went to her and said, "See if you can lure him into showing you the secret of his great strength and how we can overpower him so we may tie him up and subdue him. Each one of us will give you eleven hundred shekels of silver."

So Delilah said to Samson, "Tell me the secret of your great strength and how you can be tied up and subdued."…

Then she said to him, "How can you say, 'I love you,' when you won't confide in me? This is the third time you have made a fool of me and haven't told me the secret of your great strength." With such nagging she prodded him day after day until he was tired to death.

So he told her everything. "No razor has ever been used on my head," he said, "because I have been a Nazirite set apart to God since birth. If my head were shaved, my strength would leave me, and I would become as weak as any other man."

When Delilah saw that he had told her everything, she sent word to the rulers of the Philistines, "Come back once more; he has told me everything." So the rulers of the Philistines returned with the silver in their hands. Having put him to sleep on her lap, she called a man to shave off the seven braids of his hair, and so began to subdue him. And his strength left him.

The big effect of little choices

Samson seemed to have all the right stuff. An angel announced his birth and instructed his parents to raise him to live as a lifelong Nazirite, a person set apart by God. But Samson's privileged beginnings didn't automatically endow him with moral integrity. Over the course of his life he deliberately participated in the things he and his parents had promised not to do.

Ultimately, Samson was unable to fully realize his potential or use the gifts God had given him. This is true of many of us. Though God has uniquely gifted us for his purpose, we are unable to live up to our potential because we continually fall victim to our sinful nature.

Samson didn't turn toward sin in one grand decision. A lifetime of little choices resulted in Samson's demise. Similarly, it isn't the politician's final bribe, but rather his early career decision to bend the rules, that leads to his downfall. And it isn't the public moral failing of the religious leader, but the many unconfessed sins that preceded it, that bring him down.

So, before making what appears to be a harmless decision, stop and evaluate the cost. Success is less about having the right stuff than it is about choosing the right way.

After the death of Saul, David returned from defeating the Amalekites and stayed in Ziklag two days. On the third day a man arrived from Saul's camp, with his clothes torn and with dust on his head. When he came to David, he fell to the ground to pay him honor.

He said, "The men fled from the battle. Many of them fell and died. And Saul and his son Jonathan are dead."

Then David said to the young man who brought him the report, "How do you know that Saul and his son Jonathan are dead?"

"I happened to be on Mount Gilboa," the young man said, "and there was Saul, leaning on his spear, with the chariots and riders almost upon him. When he turned around and saw me, he called out to me, and I said, 'What can I do?'

"Then he said to me, 'Stand over me and kill me! I am in the throes of death, but I'm still alive.'

"So I stood over him and killed him, because I knew that after he had fallen he could not survive.

David took up this lament concerning Saul and his Son Jonathan ...

"I grieve for you, Jonathan my brother;
You were very dear to me.
Your love for me was wonderful,
More wonderful than that of women."

Crossing the gender gap

avid and Jonathan were alike in so many ways. Though supposedly they were rivals for the kingship of Israel, they were more like brothers. They came to be intimate friends in the royal court and likely fought together in battle. They knew each other so well that they anticipated each other's needs. So when Jonathan died in battle, David was grief stricken. He had lost his soul brother whose love, he said, was more wonderful than that of a woman.

Even today, it can sometimes be easier to relate to a person of our own gender than to relate to a spouse. That's because men and women have different needs, wants, desires and priorities, and they communicate in different ways. Instead of trying to change each other's approach, a husband and wife would do better to learn from each other.

Marriage is the primary and most vital human relationship we can have in life. Yes, we need to allow each other time to maintain friendships with people of the same gender. But the greater challenge for two who are so different is to become so strongly united that they can say to one another, "Your love for me is more wonderful than that of anyone else."

Notes

Notes

Notes

Notes

Notes

Notes

Notes

Notes

Notes

Notes

Notes

Notes

Notes

Notes

Notes